M000284136

BY GEORGE DOHRMANN

Play Their Hearts Out:
A Coach, His Star Recruit, and the Youth Basketball Machine

Superfans: Into the Heart of Obsessive Sports Fandom

Switching Fields:
Inside the Fight to Remake Men's Soccer in the United States

SWITCHING FIELDS

SWITCHING FIELDS

INSIDE THE FIGHT TO REMAKE
MEN'S SOCCER IN THE UNITED STATES

GEORGE DOHRMANN

BALLANTINE BOOKS · NEW YORK

Copyright © 2022 by George Dohrmann

All rights reserved.

Published in the United States by Ballantine Books, an imprint of
Random House, a division of Penguin Random House LLC, New York.

BALLANTINE is a registered trademark and the colophon is a
trademark of Penguin Random House LLC.

LIBRARY OF CONGRESS CATALOGING-IN-PUBLICATION DATA
Names: Dohrmann, George, author.
Title: Switching fields: inside the fight to remake men's soccer in
the United States / George Dohrmann.
Description: First edition. | New York: Ballantine Group, [2022]
Identifiers: LCCN 2022010428 (print) | LCCN 2022010429 (ebook) |
ISBN 9781524798864 (hardcover) | ISBN 9781524798871 (ebook)
Subjects: LCSH: United States Men's National Soccer Team. |
Major League Soccer (Organization) | Soccer—United States—History.
Classification: LCC GV944.U5 D64 2022 (print) |
LCC GV944.U5 (ebook) | DDC 796.3340973—dc23/eng/20220525
LC record available at https://lccn.loc.gov/2022010428
LC ebook record available at https://lccn.loc.gov/2022010429

Printed in Canada on acid-free paper

randomhousebooks.com

2 4 6 8 9 7 5 3 1

First Edition

Book design by Fritz Metsch

For Jessica, Justin,

Natalie, Audrey, Connor,

and all the kids of the Ashland Soccer Club.

I'll be at North Mountain Park with the balls and goals.

Let's go!

CONTENTS

III.   120

IV.   164

SWITCHING FIELDS

INTRODUCTION

On October 10, 2017, the United States Men's National Team (USMNT) played the combined national team of Trinidad and Tobago in Couva, Trinidad. It was the final game of World Cup qualifying, and the U.S. needed only a tie to earn a spot in the 2018 World Cup in Russia.

It had been a rocky campaign for the U.S. men, marked by the dismissal of bombastic coach Jürgen Klinsmann as the team struggled to qualify, and the return of veteran Major League Soccer (MLS) and USMNT coach Bruce Arena to replace him. The U.S. was clearly a team in transition, relying on a generation of successful but older players (among them Tim Howard, Clint Dempsey, Michael Bradley, and Matt Besler). But it had won, 4–0, against Panama four days earlier—a resounding performance against a team more talented than Trinidad and Tobago—which had already been eliminated from World Cup contention.

Going into the game, Federation Internationale de Football Association (FIFA) ranked the USMNT 28th in the world, one spot above the powerhouse team of the Netherlands. Trinidad and Tobago was ranked 99th. The U.S.

boasted a population of over 330 million people from which to draw players, and its ascending pro league, Major League Soccer, was among the top dozen leagues in the world at the time. The T&T squad, in contrast, was pulled from a pool of 1.3 million people—about the size of Dallas—and one list ranked its Pro League behind more than 130 others.

The U.S. had also qualified for every World Cup since 1990. Its region—CONCACAF, the Confederation of North, Central America and Caribbean Association Football—is far less competitive than Europe or South America, where in every cycle a few good teams miss out on the World Cup. Three teams from CONCACAF would qualify for the 2018 event in Russia, and a fourth could as well, via an inter-confederation playoff. The U.S. didn't have to finish ahead of Mexico, its rival and the region's most consistent performer; it just had to finish in the top four.

For people who follow soccer, what occurred on a soggy field at Ato Boldon Stadium in Couva was incomprehensible. An own goal by U.S. defender Omar González in the 17th minute. A shot in the 37th minute from about thirty-five yards out that a goalkeeper with Tim Howard's experience and ability should have saved. Howard blundering a shot from even farther in the 44th minute that nearly gifted T&T a third goal. Christian Pulisic, who had turned nineteen only a month earlier, scored in the 47th minute to draw the U.S. to within one, 2–1, but his goal would be the only one of the day for the Americans. Other than Pulisic, the team had played with a striking lack of energy and urgency. After the final whistle, several U.S. players just stood in shock. Pulisic crouched down, pulled his jersey over his face, and began to cry, the indelible image from the worst loss in USMNT history.

For the first time in thirty years, the U.S. would miss the World Cup.

In the aftermath, discussions of the defeat tended to follow one of two tracks. One focused on what had happened on the field in Couva, and what might have been done differently. Arena had gone with the same attack-minded team that had defeated Panama days earlier. Should he have put fresher legs on the field and perhaps played more defensively? Why start González over Geoff Cameron, a starter in England's Premier League at the time? Most sports media and fans circled around those traditional what-ifs.

The second track took a wider view. At the time of the Couva disaster, there were about seven million kids between the ages of six and seventeen playing soccer in the United States. Yet much, much smaller countries, with millions fewer kids playing the game, were considerably better at cultivating talent. How is it that, say, Uruguay (with a *total* population of 3.4 million) could produce world-class players—from Luis Suárez and Edinson Cavani to Ronald Araújo and Federico Valverde—but U.S. fans were reduced to debating whether Omar González or Geoff Cameron was a better national team starter? To focus on lineup choices or tactics in one game was to miss that the system was failing, rendering a country that should be a shark into a minnow.

And the USMNT has long been a minnow, even if the sport's power brokers in America and its most devoted fans have resisted acknowledging that fact.

After the loss at Couva, I dug up a study commissioned by the leaders of the United States Soccer Federation nearly twenty years earlier. Project 2010, as it was called, was meant to outline what it would take for the U.S. men to join the ranks of Brazil, Germany, Italy, and other global soccer powers by 2010. The cover page of the study included a photo of Neil Armstrong from the 1969 lunar landing, but with a World Cup trophy in his right hand, under the words WE CAN FLY. "Throughout history, Americans have many times demonstrated a remarkable ability to accomplish extraordinary goals," read the introduction. "While Americans do not own a monopoly on inventiveness or problem solving, one fact sets them apart from the rest of the world. America's collective resources and creativity are the greatest on earth."

The 113-page report was written by Carlos Queiroz, who coached Portugal's national team and the professional club Sporting CP in his native country and Real Madrid in Spain. He had experience at the sport's highest level, and he had also coached the New York/New Jersey MetroStars in Major League Soccer, so he was familiar with the United States and spoke English and Spanish. Queiroz and his longtime assistant coach, Dan Gaspar, traveled the country talking with the sport's stakeholders: federation officials, national team coaches, MLS coaches, youth and college coaches. The goal of the study was "to review all levels of soccer in the United States, compare it to other successful soccer countries in the world and chart a course for the future of soccer in the United States," Queiroz wrote.

Once you get past the sanguine cover image of the moon landing, it is hard to view Project 2010 as anything other than a total takedown of America's development system for male players. One page of the completed study features words in massive white type against a black background reading: PROJECT 2010 IS NOT ABOUT THE BUSINESS OF SOCCER. PROJECT 2010 IS ABOUT THE BUSINESS OF WINNING. It was a clear nod to the fact that so many of the sport's leaders in the U.S. have long acted out of self-interest, protecting their income streams at the expense of what is good for young players and the broader development system.

Queiroz delivered Project 2010 to U.S. Soccer's leaders just after the 1998 World Cup in France, and the timing was apt. The U.S. had gone winless in its group, losing to Germany, Iran, and Yugoslavia. The Iran game was particularly embarrassing, since that country was playing in only its second World Cup and first since 1978. Iranian fans celebrated late into the night in the bars of Lyon. (I drowned my sorrows alongside them, wearing a U.S. jersey; a red, white, and blue jester hat; and blue face paint.) Queiroz's report cast the Americans' flop in France in the proper light: "No one should be surprised about the performance of the U.S. team in France. It was a natural occurrence—nothing more nor less than the reality of soccer in the United States," he wrote.

The report was a bucket of ice water in the face of anyone who thought the U.S. was close to being a world soccer power. It laid out the many reasons the current developmental setup in America wasn't working. But even more powerful than Queiroz's summarized findings were the raw comments he included at the end of the study, extracts from the interviews he and Gaspar conducted with coaches and others around the country. The remarks (more than 170 of them) are unvarnished critiques of a U.S. system that in 1998, nearly twenty years before Couva, was deemed by many respondents to be an institutional mess. Among the comments:

- Soccer is politically driven by self-interest.
- The biggest issue is player development. The talent is here, but the environment is not.
- Overseas there is a clear picture. In the U.S., we are searching for a clear structure.
- We must have them in a residency program that simulates a professional experience.
- We must get MLS involved in the development process.
- It is a white, middle-class sport. In the rest of the world it is the people's sport.
- We need to mobilize and accelerate development of the entire U.S. player pool by integrating unaffiliated, principally Hispanic, youth players into the mainstream.
- In basketball, everyone wants to be [Michael] Jordan, in football everyone wants to be [Joe] Montana. In soccer, who do the kids want to be?
- The fault of the system is at the entry level. Players are being observed by inexperienced coaches.

To fix all these problems, Queiroz offered recommendations for how to restructure men's soccer in the U.S., including an overhaul of coaching and scouting networks, more connectivity between the federation and state associations, development of an academy system, and more. Taken together, the recommendations amounted to a complete re-imagining of how male players are scouted and developed. He also warned that the U.S. wouldn't find any shortcuts in the process and urged leaders to look past the successes of individual games and single events; to not find optimism where none existed. "Regardless of the national team's current results, it does not change the reality of soccer. We cannot be so naive to think that we will win on miracles," he wrote. "If I suffer from an illness, I can take medicine to reduce the pain, but it doesn't necessarily mean that I will be free of disease. Likewise, the U.S. could have a good result in the World Cup, but it might not be the best indicator of whether or not we are progressing in the right direction at all levels at home. Only when we improve all competition at the state and local levels will we raise the level of play throughout the United States. As the cream rises to the top, then and only then will we experience, in a systematic way, meaningful improvement in the results and ability of the U.S. team."

Project 2010 did not prompt a massive restructuring of soccer in America. The United States Soccer Federation did not throw massive money and resources into the sweeping overhaul that Queiroz advised. Some of the report's recommendations were gradually implemented, but they were minor. To steal Queiroz's illness metaphor: The U.S. took a couple aspirin and went about its business.

That inaction was, in no small part, because of what happened at the 2002 World Cup, where the USMNT made an improbable run to the quarterfinals. Queiroz had warned against reading too much into one set of World Cup results, and yet in 2002 the U.S. Soccer Federation did exactly that. But then the USMNT went winless at the 2006 World Cup. And at the 2010 event the U.S. was not even close to being a championship contender. It took a miracle goal against Algeria just to get out of the group stage, and then Ghana outclassed the Americans in the Round of 16. In 2014, they made the knockout stage of the World Cup but lost there to a clearly superior Belgian team. The U.S. men also failed to qualify for the Olympics in 2012 and 2016.

Reading the Project 2010 report soon after the disaster in Couva, it was hard not to view it as a missed opportunity. A respected coach had given the sport's stakeholders a blueprint for how to fix its system and begin to catch up to the rest of the world, and it had been mostly ignored. Not only was there no moon landing moment for soccer in America, the rocket never even got built.

It would have been easy, in the emotional weeks after Couva, to despair about a seemingly irreparable system and the inaction of U.S. soccer leaders, to see America's soccer future as bleak. That's where I likely would have ended up had I not, in the same month as the Couva disaster, tuned in to watch the Under-17 World Cup.

The U.S. team in that event, a group of sixteen- and seventeen-year-old boys, opened by trouncing host India, then soundly beat Ghana. The young Americans then played Colombia to a standstill before losing, but they still advanced out of the group and into the Round of 16. The U.S. had failed to qualify for the previous two U-17 World Cups, a harbinger of the U.S. senior team's future struggles, so getting past the group stage was a major accomplishment. The young U.S. team then dominated Paraguay to make the quarterfinals, where it fell to England, a team that included a host of future Premier League standouts.

As I watched the U-17s play in India, I was struck by how different this team was than the youth teams that had represented America in the past. The majority of the twenty-one players on the roster were already playing or training with professional clubs. Sergiño Dest was with Ajax in the Netherlands; Carlos Joaquim Dos Santos was with Portuguese powerhouse Benfica; Timothy Weah played for Paris Saint-Germain in France; Josh Sargent with German Bundesliga club Werder Bremen. Four of the players were in the academy at Atlanta United, an MLS team that didn't even exist until 2014. Not that long ago, the U.S. was pulling kids off high school teams to play in international youth events. Now the core of this U-17 team was made up of players already signed to a professional contract or on their way to doing so.

Another aspect of that U-17 team also caught my attention. Against India and Ghana, more than half of the starting players for the U.S. were Black or Latino. No longer was the U.S. trotting out a team of predominantly big, suburban white kids. The roster represented America's populace in a way not seen before. The quality of the play was also notable. This group of U-17s was far more skilled, far more technical with the ball, than any U.S. youth team I'd seen in the more than twenty-five years I'd closely followed the sport. Watching the players move, their understanding of the game, their ability to create space and goal-scoring opportunities, was mesmerizing. Many of the U.S. players could have been wearing the jersey of Spain or Argentina, and you wouldn't have thought them out of place.

At the exact moment that followers of U.S. men's soccer were apoplectic over the senior team's failure to qualify for the World Cup in Russia, here was a group of boys showing themselves to be the most promising collection of talent to ever emerge from the United States. As fans called for the firing of Arena, the U.S. senior team coach (he resigned), and demanded the ouster of federation president Sunil Gulati (he didn't run for reelection), and as they spoke about Couva as the bottoming-out of men's soccer in America, they likely missed the gift offered by that group of teenagers in India.

Hope.

What I saw from the U-17s cast what happened in Couva in a different light. The loss to T&T was not some sort of tipping point; it was the last gasp of the old guard, the old way, the old system. Those U-17 players and other young talents that followed in the coming years would find their way onto some of the top professional teams in the world—Chelsea, Manchester City, Bayern Munich, Borussia Dortmund, RB Leipzig, Barcelona, Juventus, Roma, and more. Soon, the U.S. development system that Queiroz found to be fragmented and inefficient would begin identifying and developing talent at such a high rate that scouts for European clubs would flock to the fields of America to look for players; some of those clubs even set up their own youth academies in the States to mine for greatness.

A number of the substantial changes Queiroz suggested in Project 2010 came around anyway—albeit not by 2010. It took years and years; it happened (somewhat) organically, in-dividuals forcing change rather than leaders leading. But it did happen. Those U-17s gliding around the field in India were proof.

To understand how that occurred, I embarked upon an exercise not unlike the one Queiroz and Gaspar did when they compiled Project 2010, talking to coaches, club direc-tors, and others around the country. The goal was to some-how map the shifting landscape of the sport, to understand what was changing and how those changes came about. That exploration took me to a suburb of Des Moines, Iowa, to meet an army veteran who spent years fighting the state soc-cer association just so marginalized kids could play the game. It took me to San Diego, where lines have long been drawn around who does and does not get access to the game. In Houston, I watched a New Jersey native who'd become a soccer icon in Japan attempt to reshape how the youngest kids get introduced to the game. In San Antonio, Texas, and Omaha, Nebraska, I encountered coaches and team officials trying to catch talented players who might otherwise slip through the cracks. In San Francisco, I visited a sports mar-keting company that reinvented itself to help Latino players. In Los Angeles and Washington, D.C., I learned what hap-pens when kids from underserved communities get the best coaching. In Arizona and Utah, I saw the present and future of elite player development.

This book is primarily about the men's development sys-tem in America—its past, present, and future—but change is also happening in the women's game. The United States Women's National Team (USWNT) has been the sport's gold standard, winners of four World Cups and four Olympic gold medals. Yet the way female players are being developed here and abroad is also evolving, a shift that the most accomplished women's coach in history believes threatens America's dominance.

To be sure, the system that develops male players in the United States is not fixed. Many problems remain. As I interviewed coaches and club directors and others, I heard many of the same criticisms listed at the end of Queiroz's report. There is much work to be done. No matter the progress, it would be unwise to point to a men's World Cup in the very near future and declare it as *the* moment that the U.S. has finally reached the level of the world's soccer superpowers.

But that day is coming, and it is not as far off as you may think.

THE AMERICAN WAY

Tailoring soccer for success in the States

The meeting took place on August 15, 1964. That much is certain.

There have been reports that it was staged in the Torrance, California, garage of one of the participants, which conjures images of men in plaid pants sitting in lawn chairs, drinking Coors from yellow pull-top cans.

Later, at least one of the participants insisted they met at a restaurant, not someone's home. Given the date, small talk may have centered on the Angels pitcher who'd just been suspended for fighting a sportswriter, or race riots in New Jersey and Illinois.

One retelling placed the meeting at a hotel near Beverly Hills, which is about as far from a Torrance garage as one can get.

The archives of the American Youth Soccer Organization

(AYSO), from which most of this chapter is drawn, are fuzzy on the details, but there is no dispute over who organized the meeting: Duncan Duff, president of the Greater Los Angeles Soccer League (GLASL). Duff was a Scotsman who had played and then coached adult teams in the area. He had led the GLASL since 1953, and he set up the meeting because he believed the Los Angeles area was ready to expand beyond adult teams. It was time to try to bring youth soccer to the Southland again.

The *again* was why Bill Hughes was Duff's first call. About eight years earlier, in 1956, Hughes, who was British, had created a youth league within the GLASL. It consisted of fourteen teams, with kids ranging in age from nine to fourteen. Teams were divided along ethnic lines—a German team, a Scottish team, a Mexican team, and so on—just like in the GLASL adult league. The number of kids on each squad was determined simply by how many signed up, meaning some teams had dozens of kids and others had just enough to field a team. No consideration was given to where the children lived; some players on the Yugoslavian team had to drive twenty miles to practice.

Halfway through that 1956 season, Hughes asked for a "special meeting" to discuss the youth league's future. Youth soccer in the GLASL was doomed, he told league leaders. Coaches and referees were dropping out, refusing to make the long commutes. Players who were riding the bench all game were quitting. He hadn't gotten the numbers he wanted because some kids refused to be part of "ethnic" teams. Scores were too lopsided.

He suggested that the GLASL radically rethink their approach to youth soccer, and offered four proposals:

- *Only fifteen players maximum per team.* This would eliminate situations like the time a team showed up with thirty-three players and its opponent had only seven.
- *Every player must play at least twenty minutes of each half.* The league had seen too many kids quit because they didn't get to play.
- *Eliminate ethnic names for teams.* Some kids (or their parents) were refusing to join teams called Scots or Magyars or Croats.
- *Keep teams within ten miles of a central point.* This would eliminate the lengthy travel that caused coaches and referees to quit.

The leadership of the GLASL didn't have the appetite to remake youth soccer. Six weeks later, at the end of the season, Hughes's youth league folded.

Eight years later, Duff wanted to give it another try, and he asked Hughes to spearhead the effort. Hughes said he would get involved only if he had allies open to rethinking how to sell the game to American families. Hughes's GLASL experience taught him that just throwing the sport in front of Americans and hoping they saw its appeal wasn't going to cut it. You had to present soccer to them, craft the experience, in a way that made it seem less foreign. Hughes and others would refer to this as having to "Americanize" the sport. It was a core belief, a guiding principle. They talked openly and often about doing soccer "The American Way," which meant adopting the changes Hughes suggested.

Duff also contacted Hans Stierle, who had gotten a small soccer program off the ground in South San Gabriel but had recently moved to Torrance. Steve Erdos, Ralph Acosta, and Ted McLean were also brought in, all of them involved in local adult soccer in some way, all of them eager to grow the game in the area.

For the meeting at the Torrance restaurant (or the garage, or the hotel) Hughes brought with him a document outlining the changes he had tried to make to the GLASL's youth league years earlier. He asked the men to commit to bringing those changes to the new league.

They all agreed that the league should not be affiliated with the GLASL. Best to start fresh, without that association. Names for this new endeavor were bandied about; at one point they settled on Southern California Junior Soccer League. But then Hughes argued that they should think bigger, try to form something that could go national. It would need a name that reflected that ambition.

Hughes was a logical choice for this new organization's first president, but when Erdos nominated him, Hughes declared that it would be "our first and last mistake." He said he was "too typically British to be the head of an American organization."

That ruled out Erdos (a Romanian) and Acosta (Mexican) and McLean (Scottish)—leaving Stierle. He had spent a large portion of his life in Germany, his parents' native country, and his given name was, well, Hans. But he was born in the United States, and that mattered above all else. The front-

facing leader, the man families would look to as they pondered letting a child try soccer, had to be seen as a "real"
American.

With Stierle as president and the others filling out the
remaining board positions, the men left the gathering at
around 10:00 P.M. AYSO, which would become perhaps the
most influential youth soccer organization in U.S. history,
was conceived in about ninety minutes.

The South Bay of Los Angeles in the 1960s was as ideal a
place as any in the U.S. to start a soccer league. In 1962, the
Los Angeles Air Force Base opened in El Segundo on the site
of what had once been an aircraft factory. There, the U.S.
would create the satellites and missiles it stockpiled in its
effort to keep ahead of Soviet efforts to do the same. Around
the base, aerospace companies flush with lucrative defense
contracts drew skilled workers to the area. The population of
El Segundo and the nearby beach cities more than doubled,
to around 125,000 by 1965, and many of the people buying
the bungalows and cottages in the area were families from
Europe who arrived with a love of soccer.

The coaches and referees of the first AYSO league, created in Torrance by Stierle, were mostly foreign-born, and
many of the players that made up the initial teams were their
children (including Stierle's own kids). But Stierle also recruited locals with no soccer exposure. He once interrupted
a softball game at a local field and asked the kids to try kick-
ing a ball around with him. Some liked it enough to join his
new league.

The first AYSO game was held February 13, 1965, at

Jefferson Elementary in Torrance—across the street from Stierle's house. Bill Hughes's guidelines meant to "Americanize" the sport had clearly been followed. The two teams were called the Bulldogs and the Hornets, a far cry from Scots and Croats. Stierle broke the game into four quarters, making it easier to track playing time so that every kid played at least a quarter. And much attention was paid to the parents; they were encouraged to volunteer and be right on the sideline, cheering away.

The second game, a week later—the Firefighters vs. the Panthers—was equally well-executed and well-received. (One player on the Firefighters was a twelve-year-old from Torrance, Siegfried "Sigi" Schmid, the son of German immigrants. He would go on to play at UCLA, coach UCLA to three NCAA men's soccer titles, win the MLS Cup as coach of the Columbus Crew, and retire in 2018 as the winningest coach in MLS history.) Two weeks later, Erdos staged a game in Culver City, the first contest in the AYSO league he formed there.

This is how soccer grew in Southern California, with the original AYSO board members seeding the game in certain areas and it spreading from there. AYSO soon expanded to Northern California and then to other states. In its first year, the organization registered 125 players. By its fifth, it had 1,830. In the 1973–74 season, AYSO's tenth year, its players numbered 26,340. It helped that AYSO soccer was a relatively inexpensive endeavor. As an early AYSO treasurer told a local newspaper: "A soccer team can be field[ed] for the cost of outfitting one [American] football player." In the first few years, the cost to register a player was $5. It eventually rose to $7, but

AYSO was transparent about how it got to that number: $2 to medical insurance, $3 to equipment and operations (like field rental), $1 to AYSO national headquarters for operations. And $1 to a fund that promoted soccer in new areas.

With each passing year, Hughes's vision and Stierle's work to Americanize soccer became more and more ingrained. An early draft of AYSO rules included a provision that "the use of a language other than English by a coach, official or participant during AYSO competition or activity shall not be permitted." (It's unclear if this was enforced.) A 1969 AYSO radio commercial stated, "Soccer is fun—but soccer American-style is more fun." The "American style" of soccer included balancing teams, another feature born in Torrance. When coaches gathered to pick from the registered players, they were told beforehand that the team they were choosing would not be the one they would coach. Thus, they were incentivized to competitively balance the squads. The completed teams were numbered, and coaches blindly drew a number and were assigned that team.

AYSO also promoted the sport as safe and healthy for kids. Unlike baseball, it would require kids to run and run. "Playing soccer is tantamount to being 'in shape,'" read a 1966 AYSO promotional poster.

AYSO surely benefited from the fact that most parents knew little about soccer. In news articles at the time, parents commented on how, at Little League baseball games, every dad in the stands had played growing up. That made for an intense environment as games unfolded on the field. But at early soccer games, ignorance was bliss. And because teams were kept local, practices and games had a neighborly vibe.

The dads coaching and refereeing lived close to one another; they worked for the same companies; their kids went to the same schools. Wives socialized on the sidelines and then delivered orange slices to the kids at halftime. Hans Stierle's wife, Christel, would be recognized as the first "soccer mom." Unintentional or not, AYSO connected the game to the nuclear family and traditional gender roles.

If you read the *Los Angeles Times* in the late 1960s, you'd find articles about hooliganism at European soccer matches. And, at the adult league games between "ethnic" teams elsewhere in Southern California, multiple languages were shouted on the pitch and on the sidelines; the players were physical, the competition fierce. In contrast, AYSO parents went to a local field on a Saturday morning with friends and neighbors, and supported the kids during a balanced game in which every child got a chance to shine, and then everyone left safe and happy.

Almost exactly one year after the meeting that birthed AYSO, the Watts riots broke out, leading to six days of unrest and thirty-four deaths. The white flight from Huntington Park, South Gate, and nearby areas pushed more families into the South Bay and other suburbs. It also created a desire for exactly what AYSO was selling: *Come try this safe sport, on teams made up of kids and parents just like you, who live near you.* For parents looking for homogeneity, it could be found on the soccer field.

Stierle and AYSO leaders made other decisions that helped further "Americanize" the sport. One example: Stierle recognized that Americans were attached to their institutions, particularly local high schools. Rather than follow the U.S.

Soccer Federation and sanction teams of high school–aged kids, AYSO cut off teams at U-16 and then later after eighth grade, allowing AYSO players and parents to migrate to the high school sports teams that were at the center of many communities. Those families then helped drive the rapid increase in high school soccer programs in California during the 1970s and '80s.

Unquestionably, AYSO leaders succeeded in making the sport more embraceable by suburban families in Southern California and beyond. Thousands upon thousands of boys (and later girls) across the country would be introduced to the sport each year via their local AYSO league, including future U.S. men's and women's national team stars like Eric Wynalda, Landon Donovan, Julie Foudy, and Alex Morgan.

Anyone who cares about soccer in the U.S. would consider what AYSO did, on balance, a net positive. But when the choice was made to do it "The American Way," to root soccer in the suburbs and tailor it for the people who clustered there, it sent soccer in the United States on a path that would limit its potential—even as the sport was experiencing significant growth.

THE DIVIDING LINE

The rise of youth club soccer, and who was left behind

Not long after AYSO leaders "Americanized" soccer and moved it into the suburbs, ambitious parents decided they wanted more for their young players. After watching their children excel in the sport, dominating their local AYSO league, they wondered if there wasn't something more for them to aspire to than a plastic participation trophy and postseason party at Shakey's Pizza. They wanted more training. More and better competition. And because AYSO was born in the suburbs, its league populated mostly with kids from middle- to upper-middle-class families, these ambitious parents had the means to pay far more than the $5 that AYSO initially charged for a season.

This is how it has gone with most youth sports in America: parents with money ratcheting up the emphasis and the stakes. And once the desire is there, it isn't long before people recognize they can profit off it. Parents who want "more" for their child, especially ones who don't know the sport or what exactly "more" looks like, make the best customers.

In the late 1970s and early '80s, the first private youth soccer clubs were founded in California. Such clubs existed already on the East Coast, but the spread in California was swift and pervasive, an industry popping up that quickly changed the game nationwide. These clubs purported to offer exactly what parents sought—better coaching and stiffer competition—and they also hosted and traveled to tournaments, providing a way for parents to measure their children's abilities against kids from different areas. The kumbaya soccer of AYSO, the neighborhood leagues, didn't go away, but running parallel to that recreational soccer was a more serious and expensive version, and it wasn't long before it was the dominant form of youth soccer, at least for families "serious" about the game.

As you move through America's youth soccer development system, you quickly get familiar with a term: "Pay-to-Play." It refers to youth clubs that have become such a source of revenue that they begin to act like a big business—and thus don't always operate in the best interests of the kids or the youth soccer ecosystem as a whole. The stated goal of the U.S. Soccer Federation (USSF) is to get as many kids as possible playing, to deepen the pool of talent. But at the local level, the clubs control the sport. The structure of registration fees, the salaries of coaches and others, the amount of scholarship money (if any) given out, all of that is determined by the clubs. For decades, the USSF and the state associations have, largely, worked in service of these big youth clubs.

If you search a nonprofit database and plug in the names of youth clubs around the country, you'll find many that bring in millions of dollars in revenue and have reserve funds running into six figures. You'll find executive directors who make hundreds of thousands of dollars a year, directors of coaching who do the same, and treasurers who make nearly twice the median salary for the area in which the club is located. There are clubs that could provide scholarships for every kid in the club and barely scratch the surface of their cash on hand. Keep digging, and you'll find that many of those clubs give out less in scholarships than they spend on referee fees.

Running a soccer club is not easy; coaching kids and managing parents is no walk in the park. But when critics of America's system point to Pay-to-Play as the main reason the U.S. has failed to produce elite players, they have, well, a point. Many clubs have a significant bottom line to meet, and over the years their actions have moved in the service of meeting it. This is most noticeable in the cost of participation, those registration fees. A 2017 study by Utah State researchers found that U.S. families spend on average $1,472 per year for a child to play soccer, with some paying as much as $5,500. (That survey included families of recreational and elite players and those with children as young as eight.)

In 2019, famed Swedish forward Zlatan Ibrahimović, upon leaving Los Angeles (where he played two seasons with the L.A. Galaxy of Major League Soccer), told *GQ Italy* that while living in Southern California he had paid around $7,000 per year for his sons, ages eleven and thirteen, to play soccer. "It has to be said that the sport is expensive, very expensive," Zlatan said. "For example, in order for my children to play in a good football team, I have to pay $3,500 per child. . . . I dislike it very much because not everyone has the money needed and the sport should be something for everyone."

Ibrahimović may be wealthy now, but he didn't grow up with money. Experiencing America's youth soccer setup after years immersed in Europe's egalitarian development was jarring. In most of the rest of the world, soccer is accessible to all children, no matter where they live or their socioeconomic status. In the U.S., it gradually became readily available only to kids who lived in a certain place (the suburbs), and who were from the most affluent families.

What impact did this have on America's ability to develop elite players?

David Keyes didn't set out to answer that question when, in 2011, he began to study the youth soccer scene in San Diego. He was in his sixth year as a student in the anthropology program at the University of California San Diego. He had already earned a master's degree; for his master's project, Keyes studied people who had migrated to nontraditional places, like those from Central Mexico who ended up living near his Ohio hometown. For six of his eight years at UCSD, he worked with the Mexican Migration Field Research Program. He would go to small towns in Mexico in January and stay there for ten days, trying to survey everyone above sixteen years old.

Keyes had long been fascinated by immigration. Learning how his grandmother on his mother's side immigrated to the United States from Ukraine may have planted a seed. He also played soccer while growing up near Dayton. "It was pretty rough-and-tumble soccer, not very elegant. It was coached by kids' dads who hadn't played the game," Keyes says. At Earlham College, a Division III school in Richmond, Indiana, Keyes was just good enough to walk onto the soccer team. "We happened to be really good the two years I was there, so I can say I rode the bench on a top-ten D-III team," he says.

When it came time to choose a topic for his doctoral thesis, Keyes ended up marrying his interests in immigration and soccer. Sports have historically been held up as "a panacea to social problems, including immigrant assimilation," Keyes wrote in his thesis. Political scientist Robert Putnam suggested that sports "can foster connections between diverse people who might not otherwise interact," and Keyes aimed to prove whether, in the world of youth soccer, that was true.

Some people are quick to dismiss academic exercises like the one Keyes set out on in 2011. But here was a highly trained cultural anthropologist turning his focus upon American soccer. And contrary to stereotypes of academics, he would not do so by reading stacks of papers. Keyes was a researcher, and he would go into the field, spending eighteen months immersed in the San Diego youth soccer scene.

Montgomery-Waller Community Park covers twenty-five acres just west of the I-805 freeway in Chula Vista, California. In the Latino community, the park is often referred to as *"Ala,"* the Spanish word for "wing," because of the park's signature feature: a 93-foot stainless steel airplane wing mounted so it faces upward, like a shark fin. The wing was dedicated in 1950 to honor the achievements of pioneering local aviator John J. Montgomery.

When Keyes began his research, he first thought he would volunteer to coach a team. "But I was this guy calling up, not married, without any children, asking to coach a team," he recalled. "That wasn't going to happen." So he looked for clubs that would allow him to hang around their teams and families. Three eventually agreed, and he set out to study them in a manner that, as he wrote in his dissertation, would strike many as odd:

> Conducting ethnographic fieldwork on youth soccer involved no multi-day treks to tiny villages on distant islands. It included no moment of acceptance into a community after a shared experience of harassment from outsiders. It mostly consisted of me, standing on the sidelines of youth soccer fields, talking with parents and coaches. I got there by traversing the highways of San Diego in my 2004 Honda Civic. I like to think that I was "accepted" by my informants, but as a "father without a son," I'm not sure that I ever became more than a slightly odd figure with an inexplicably strong interest in their child's soccer team.

One of Keyes's research bases was *Ala*. Beneath that towering silver wing were uneven, pockmarked fields, a mix of dirt patches and tired grass that barely resembled the fields Keyes had played on growing up in Ohio. This was the home field of the Aztecs Futbol Club, founded in 1991.

At the time Keyes began his research, the population of Chula Vista was 58 percent Latino, unsurprising since the park sits about five miles from the U.S.–Mexico border. But on any given day, the players on the fields, and the coaches and parents on the sidelines, were by Keyes's estimate 90 percent Latino. The families that made up the Aztecs FC worked in construction and landscaping; they cleaned homes. The median salary in the area was around $39,000.

Keyes spent countless hours at the park. He visited with coaches and families elsewhere—in their homes, in local restaurants, and in the community—but the majority of his time examining the lives of the players and coaches and parents of the Aztecs FC was at the fields. One winter evening, as the sun set and the sky darkened, the lights suddenly went out during the middle of a practice. When, after a long spell, the lights didn't turn back on, a group of twelve- and thirteen-year-old boys ran up the hill to the park office, shouting at those inside to please, please turn the lights back on. They walked away, dejected, ready to depart, when suddenly the light came back. Keyes would later reflect on that moment, writing:

> It was never clear on that night why the lights had gone out. But in many ways, this uncertainty is emblematic of the plight of the club as a whole. Though it undoubtedly has many talented players, the club lacks the financial resources to really succeed in the ultra

competitive world of Southern California youth soccer. In the best of times, [Aztecs FC] teams play on
bumpy, sloped, dirt-pocked fields; in the worst of
times, the lights go out on them.

About 35 miles north of *Ala,* in the tony San Diego suburb of Del Mar, was Keyes's second research site: the Polo
Fields. Tucked into the San Dieguito Valley west of Interstate 5, eighty acres of the fields, which were then owned by
the San Diego Polo Club, had been converted to twenty soccer
fields. Lush and green, sitting up against the San Dieguito
River, it would be hard to find a prettier plot of land to host a
youth soccer game.

The Polo Fields were the home of the San Diego Surf, one
of the biggest and most successful soccer clubs in America
since its founding in 1978.

Each year, the Surf sent players off to college soccer, and
several professionals had come out of the club. At the Polo
Fields, Keyes watched as Jaguars and BMW sedans and expensive SUVs rolled up and dropped off the kids. On those
beautiful fields, they would line up their identical club back-
packs in a perfect row, slip on the newest model of cleats,
and then take the field in matching training attire.

There are no lights at the Polo Fields, but had there been,
it would be safe to say they'd never go out on *these* kids.

At the time Keyes took up his post at the Polo Fields, Del
Mar was about 91 percent white, and the average income in
the city was $138,000. There were a few Latino players on
the Surf's best teams, but otherwise the players were white
or non-Latino.

The third club that Keyes examined was the Nomads, a well-known organization in La Jolla that since 1976 has produced top players, among them former men's national team captain Steve Cherundolo. Despite the many talented players that have flowed through the club, the Nomads had become, in the San Diego soccer ecosystem, something like a middle-class club. They had started out like the Surf—a predominantly white club—but had purposely moved in a different direction, diversifying to the point that in some years the club's best teams featured zero kids from La Jolla.

In 2012, the year Keyes was deep into his research, the revenue for the trio of clubs he followed looked like this:

Surf: $2 million
Nomads: $607,000
Aztecs: $172,000

Another way to look at the financial differences among the three clubs: The Surf and Nomads were operated by individuals for whom running the club was their primary job. The head of the Aztecs made his living as a landscaper.

In 2012, the annual registration fee for a Surf player was around $1,600; the Nomads fee was about $1,300; Aztecs FC charged $10 a week. Keyes saw Aztecs FC families ask for extensions to cover even that small amount; one good player had to quit the club after his father lost his construction job. And the $10 a week was just an entry cost; it didn't cover equipment, travel, or other expenses that families in the suburban clubs absorbed without a quibble.

The Surf and Nomads occupied some of the same space—

their teams regularly faced one another in local leagues—but the Aztecs existed in a different world. Most of their teams played in a league known locally as "the Mexican League," unaffiliated with the state association or U.S. Soccer—and though occasionally a team would save up enough money to travel to an elite tournament, that was typically a once-a-year opportunity. They played on substandard fields and with lesser equipment. Their coaches, while undeniably knowledgeable, went unpaid, and did not have the same relationships with college coaches and other influencers as the coaches of the Surf and Nomads.

These different worlds of soccer weren't specific to San Diego. In 2011, the year Keyes started his research, youth and college soccer in America was being played mostly by the affluent. The largest group of "core" players (who played twenty-six or more times a year) came from families earning $100,000 or more annually, according to data compiled by what was then called the Sporting Goods Manufacturers Association. Almost 79 percent of the most dedicated players came from households earning $50,000 or more. And the more money a family made, the more likely its child was to start playing soccer at a younger age. (In more recent studies, those trends have continued.) As Keyes observed: "There are two separate but intertwined worlds of soccer, with one clearly of a higher status than the other. And there are two separate but intertwined sectors of the economy, with an identical status differential."

Early AYSO leaders, as they mapped out "The American Way," did not intentionally exclude Latino players and their parents from participating. Many were immigrants themselves, after all. But most were from Europe, and soccer at that time in the U.S. was considered more of a European sport than a Latino one. It is unsurprising then that when the newly formed suburban clubs went to look for "experts" in the sport they turned to coaches from Europe (mostly the United Kingdom), creating a system where (white) European expertise became seen as most valuable.

In the 1980s, as Pay-to-Play clubs proliferated, ties to Great Britain became a selling point, with clubs touting coaches and club directors from overseas. Soccer clubs and camps still promote their associations with Europe, often branding themselves as "British" or "English." Challenger Sports, which was founded in 1985 (and at the time called British Soccer Camps), markets itself as "the largest soccer camp company in North America" and still offers its "British" soccer camps in cities and towns across the United States. It is a sort of traveling soccer carnival of coaches. For many parents who sign up their children, a British accent automatically equals expertise.

In many parts of the U.S., a soccer association with England or Ireland or Scotland or Wales is still considered more credible (and marketable) than, say, a connection to Mexico. "There is, of course, a racial component to that, what is considered a valuable foreignness," Keyes says.

One can understand how this two-class system developed, but why did it persist? Why were Latino players so marginalized that entire clubs have had to be created to serve them?

Some of the answers can be found by digging deeper into the Nomads, that third club that Keyes followed, one that has tried to assimilate Latino players into its program and has both succeeded and failed because of it.

Derek Armstrong is believed to be the first full-time, paid coach in U.S. youth soccer, a tricky designation to fact-check but one that hasn't been refuted. He arrived from England, having coached teams at various levels there. When he took over the Nomads in 1981, he created the model of multiple teams at cascading age levels (U-15, U-14, U-13, etc.) that now can be found at youth clubs across the country. In 1991, his son, David, also joined the Nomads staff; the father-son combination would remake the club and heavily influence youth soccer in California.

The Nomads won big early in Derek Armstrong's tenure, but trips to the Dallas Cup, the prestigious tournament that attracts youth teams from all over the world, opened his and David's eyes to the disparity in talent between the best Nomad teams and those in the rest of the world. Theirs was a club that would produce national team players Cherundolo, Jovan Kirovski, and Frankie Hejduk, but the Armstrongs— David in particular—determined that the Nomads' teams of mostly suburban white kids weren't good enough to compete against the best teams in the world.

Around 1992, David began aggressively recruiting kids who lived south of the Nomads' base in La Jolla, players from Chula Vista and the surrounding areas. Player by player, he put together a team that would win a state championship as U-11s and return to the Dallas Cup as U-12s. That team hung with a South American team that would have steamrolled the earlier iteration of the Nomads.

By 2002, when David gave an interview to *Soccer America* detailing the club's move toward including more Latino players, there were no players from La Jolla on a Nomads team that competed at the Dallas Cup. "I like the blend we've got," David said of the team's racial diversity. "The Caucasian kids are generally taller, more physical, more dominant in the air, and you need that, too." He described the Nomads' playing style as "taking a bit of the English game, a bit of the South American game, and putting it all together."

Three decades ago, when the Nomads—one of the most influential youth soccer clubs in America—made a move into the Latino community and found almost instant success, it could have changed the way clubs operated throughout Southern California and across the country.

But it didn't. At least not significantly. The reason has little to do with what happened on the field.

An unspoken truth about large suburban soccer clubs is that the recreational players and players on the "B" and "C" competitive teams pay full freight, subsidizing the scholarship players on the top teams. While Keyes tracked the Nomads, its enrollment at the rec level was going down, and tournament revenue was also drying up. Parents who had been able to pay full registration fees were leaving for other clubs where they thought their children might play more. Other parents were less generous about stepping up when small costs arose for needy families. It was becoming harder and harder to sustain a model that subsidized a large number of Latino players with scholarships. Fielding teams and getting them to games across the West had become too expensive.

Keyes watched as several Latino players, no longer able to afford the fees, left one of the Nomads' top teams, replaced by white kids who could pay the entire cost. The Nomads had around fifteen boys' teams in 2012, with its oldest teams just under 70 percent Latino. The Surf, meanwhile, had nearly seventy teams, and its oldest squads were 38 percent Latino. One local coach described the Surf to Keyes as "leche with a tinge of café"—milk with a tinge of coffee. "The typical mechanism is that they'll have thirteen Anglo guys who are going to pay and two [Latino] scholarship guys. One will score the goals and the other is the playmaker," a coach told Keyes. That the Surf was more judicious with its scholarships could be seen as smart, if the goal was to sustain its business model. As Keyes noted, "By prioritizing the financial position of the club, [the Surf] has, implicitly if not explicitly, made its choice about the integration of Latino players. And that choice is to remain a mostly white, mostly affluent, suburban club."

Some Latinos *were* getting to play for the Surf and the Nomads and other suburban clubs, being seen by pro and college coaches, stepping over the dividing line and reaping some benefits. But not enough of them were getting that opportunity, Keyes found, and it was also a system riddled with flaws. First, the scholarships could be pulled at any time. If a kid had a bad season, it could mean a ticket back to *Ala,* and that put immense pressure on young players. It was also no secret who the scholarship kids were, a stigma that led to the term "mercs" (as in paid mercenaries) being hurled at some Latino players. There were also expenses that the scholarships didn't cover, like travel to tournaments. Not every Latino family needed help paying the extra costs, but one coach told Keyes of how an offer of an extra training session for only five dollars had been rejected because too few of the scholarship families could afford it.

Finally, moving to one of the suburban clubs was a massive cultural adjustment that some players and their families just couldn't handle. Many Latino players were used to communicating with their coaches and teammates in Spanish, and as a result would cluster with the only other Latinos on the team (a clear blow to Robert Putnam's premise of sports encouraging immigrant assimilation). In Chula Vista, Keyes watched as parents arrived to deliver their kids to practice. It was often done by the fathers, he noted, and they stuck around. Groups of fathers, five or six, would huddle, chat, comment on the practice as it played out. With the suburban teams, expensive vehicles would drop the players off and pull away. That scholarship kid from Chula Vista was used to the fathers and mothers being around, and now that was gone, another cultural hurdle he would need to overcome.

After spending eighteen months with the teams, Keyes would conclude that the social interactions Putnam believed sports like youth soccer created were blunted by those economic and cultural factors. The scholarship system didn't really act as a pathway for Latino players into the youth soccer ecosystem, nor did playing youth soccer significantly aid in the assimilation process of immigrants into society at large, as Putnam believed.

In recent years, individuals and organizations have emerged to diminish the influence of some of the big suburban clubs and bring more Latino players into the U.S. system (more on that later), but even if the model is changing, it has done decades of harm.

Up until recently, the descriptors used by people in other countries to describe the U.S. men's national team—"athletic" and "industrious" and "hardworking"—were nice ways of not saying the harsh part out loud: The U.S. featured far too many players lacking elite ball skills.

That was, in part, a result of the dividing line. The U.S. has always had a large pool from which to draw those creative players, but it embraced a system that marginalized them. Latino players were priced out, relegated to pockmarked fields with tired grass, worried that at any minute the lights would go out. They were left out of the view of decision-makers, the technical directors, the scouts for pro teams, those who pick national team rosters and award college scholarships. This setup not only kept the U.S. talent pool shallow, it negated the influence Latino culture might have had on the way the U.S. played. Soccer has, at times, been compared to jazz: structured but in its highest form bursting with improvisation. The U.S. has been making music; it just decided not to invite the horn section to the stage.

At the 2014 World Cup, the last tournament the U.S. qualified for before the disaster in Couva, the roster of twenty-three players taken to Brazil included only a single Latino player. Carlos Bocanegra grew up in Upland, California, the son of a white mother and Mexican father who were both teachers. Bocanegra's youth club, Rancho Cucamonga United, was not the Surf, but it was even farther from Aztecs FC. (Bocanegra's coach was Bill Swartz, the longtime coach of the Division III program at Pomona-Pitzer Colleges.) Bocanegra was a fine player, a left-footed defender, but he was not the kind of player you make beautiful music with.

The only player on the 2014 World Cup team universally described as a creative player was Clint Dempsey. He was a middle-class white kid raised in Nacogdoches, Texas, but he learned to play with flair, cultivating a willingness "to try shit," as former USMNT coach Bruce Arena once put it.

Where did Dempsey learn to play that way?

In Nacogdoches's "Mexican League."

I

In the summer of 1985, when thirteen-year-old Matt Carver stepped off the train at Ninety-sixth Street in East Harlem, he had the goal of any kid about to be dropped into a new, strange place:

Just don't stand out *too* much.

That would be an uphill climb. A day earlier, Matt had gone with his mother to a Manhattan shoe store and procured a pair of Air Jordan 1s with money he had been saving up since Christmas. Red and black, the first of Michael Jordan's signature shoes, they were the hottest sneaker on the planet. Matt's joy and pride over those shoes radiated off him as he and his mother and three siblings walked alongside densely packed brick and stone buildings, and passed bustling bodegas (a word Matt would use for the first time that day). In his mind, the coolness of the shoes on his feet would make him a welcome addition to any crowd.

But the farther Matt and his family walked north along Third Avenue, the more it dawned on him that fitting in wouldn't be so easy. Matt was from Urbandale, Iowa, a suburb of Des Moines with a population then of about 17,000 people. It was more than 97 percent white. The slice of Harlem they'd traveled to was overwhelmingly Latino and Black. Matt was a suburban kid who on a normal summer day would be riding his 10-speed Schwinn to Brian Wilkinson's house to play H-O-R-S-E on the basketball hoop in his driveway. Or he and Brian would ride their bikes to the Hy-Vee and split the cost of a banana cream pie. They'd "test out" video games at a local computer store, never to be bothered by the clerk. They'd sneak onto the Urbandale Golf and Country Club grounds and fish for bass in a pond.

Now, he and his new Jordan 1s were standing at the corner of Third Avenue and Ninety-seventh Street, taking in the full expanse of the George Washington Houses—fourteen red-brick buildings clustered between 97th and 104th Streets. Built in 1957, the massive public housing project was unlike anything Carver had seen before. All but one of the buildings stood fourteen stories high, and they housed 1,411 apartments in total. He was a long way from Iowa.

How thirteen-year-old Matt landed on that corner takes some unpacking.

Years earlier, his parents, Victoria and Mike, had what could be called a goal-setting meeting, a discussion over what kind of children they wanted to raise. Over breakfast at an Urbandale café, they wrote their hopes for their children's futures down on paper. *Do well in school* was on the list, as was *Be kind to others*, along with other wishes parents typically hold. Then, on a piece of paper, Victoria also wrote: *Be at home and have friendships with people of other races and backgrounds and economic status.*

For Victoria and Mike, this was not some righteous-sounding promise, the kind of thing you say mostly because you want others to hear it. Mike had served on the Urbandale city council and volunteered with several local organizations. Victoria had for years worked at the childcare center in Des Moines started by Evelyn Davis, the local civils rights leader, and she helped start a computer center in the city's Black neighborhood that taught computing skills to adults and children. By 1985, when they landed in East Harlem, the Carver children had already volunteered at that computer center in Iowa and were accustomed to Victoria taking them to neighborhoods unlike the leafy, quiet streets of Urbandale.

But East Harlem was no day trip. After Victoria and Mike divorced, Victoria took a position with a nonprofit organization and moved to Brooklyn. She made the leap, leaving Urbandale and her kids, but that note, which she kept in a drawer in her desk, was still more than just words. So Mike and Victoria agreed that the kids would spend most of the summer with her. They would live in her tiny flat in Brooklyn, and their days would be spent at the Washington Houses, helping in the computer center Victoria was tasked with maintaining in one of the building's basements. If they weren't there, they'd be outside playing with kids decidedly unlike their friends back in Iowa.

In Urbandale, Matt played soccer, his favorite sport, at a park where half a dozen pristine grassy fields were lined up next to each other. His first coach was the dad of one of his teammates, who coached in jeans and tennis shoes and knew very little about the game, a typical AYSO coach. In East Harlem, there was no soccer, no coaches. Kids played stickball on the barren patches of dirt between the buildings. Still, Matt loved it. Loved the noise of it. The fierce competition. At the Washington Houses, kids played to win at every moment.

It was on the stickball field that Matt got to know Ivan. Most of the kids Matt encountered were Puerto Rican, but Ivan was Black. He was wiry and strong and good at stickball, so that made him a draw, and Matt liked how interested he was in the computers and software Victoria was introducing to the kids in that basement. "He was really inquisitive," Matt says. "And a lot of kids would run their mouth, but not him. He always gave a lot of thought to what he was going to say, and I think I was the same way."

Ivan and the other kids often asked Matt about his pigs and cows. No matter how often Matt reminded them that he lived in a house in a suburb, they teased him about being a farmer. He got to know a few of the kids well enough that he was invited into their apartments in the Washington Houses, ate meals with them. He cobbled together money and went with them to the bodegas, buying candy and grape drink. Older kids would send him to the bodega to buy them a "loosie," a single cigarette. Victoria essentially let him and his siblings run free, allowing them to be one of the children of the Washington Houses. If she had shielded her kids in any way, kept them by her side, it would have defeated the reason they were there.

Interwoven with the fun moments, the stickball and the candy runs, were the sights and sounds of a community full of people struggling. Drugs, of course. Matt saw them and was offered them. One of the older boys carried a revolver on occasion. Matt and his younger brother, Tim, visited Jose, a boy they grew to know, at Mt. Sinai Hospital in East Harlem after he was slashed multiple times across the back—wounds requiring 160 stitches—during a dispute over which group of kids would get to use the concrete playground for a game. Single-parent homes. Sparse refrigerators and not enough food on the table. He didn't process it all then, as a thirteen-year-old, but he did understand that these kids, just like him in so many ways, were also *not* like him.

In the school year after his first summer in Harlem, Matt was tapped to move into his Iowa school's program for "gifted" students. His older sister had been in that group, so Matt's invitation was not a surprise, though Matt had to work harder for it than she did. He was asked to join later than his sister had been, mostly due to some struggles in reading and writing. It meant he had spent more time with kids not labeled as exceptional.

For a child to move into the gifted program, their teacher, guardian, *and* the child all had to agree to the arrangement. When Matt's parents sat him down to deliver the news of his advancement, he pondered it for a moment and then said he wanted to stay with his current class, with the "regular" kids. As Victoria pressed him for an explanation, Matt talked about a kid in his class, a quiet Southeast Asian boy who had only lived in the U.S. for about two years. "He's as smart as me," Matt explained. "But the teachers just don't know how to teach him. When I explain the work to him, he gets it right away." He was only thirteen, but Matt recognized a system that pushed him upward over a peer because the adults hadn't found a way for both of them to rise.

Victoria moved back to Des Moines in 1986, so the trips to Harlem stopped after two summers. On his last visit there, Matt had the kids he played stickball with sign a ball, young kids scribbling their names on the rubber. For years after, Matt would find that ball on a shelf or in a box and turn it around in his hand, looking at those names, wondering what had happened to Ivan and the others.

TRADING PLACES

Why are there so few Black soccer players in America?

On December 5, 1971, in the Orange Bowl in Miami, St. Louis University and Howard University met in the NCAA men's soccer national championship game.

St. Louis University was a powerhouse. From 1959 (the year the first NCAA Championship for soccer was staged) to 1970, the Billikens won eight national championships. Their success was due in no small part to how the "Americanization" of soccer had helped the sport take hold in St. Louis. The Billikens' all-white team was entirely homegrown, bucking the growing trend at the time of colleges importing players from Europe and elsewhere. Their coach was Harry Keough, a native of St. Louis who had served in the Navy and then played for the U.S. national team in its famous 1–0 victory over England in the 1950 World Cup. Coming into the matchup, Keough's team had not lost in forty-four consecutive games.

Down the sideline from Keough was Howard coach Lincoln Phillips, a native of Trinidad. He became the first Black man to coach an American professional team in 1968, when he was a player and coach for the Washington Darts. After that team moved into the National American Soccer League in 1970, he started in goal and was named an all-star. Then Phillips, about to turn thirty, left to coach at Howard, where the pay was better and he could take classes tuition-free. (He would earn bachelor's and master's degrees from the school.) Phillips quickly turned Howard, a historically Black university, into an elite team. He brought in students from Caribbean and African nations, many of whom grew up playing in the street.

The 1971 NCAA Championship game was, as Gwilym Brown wrote in *Sports Illustrated,* one "of multiple contrasts— not just cheeky newcomer vs. entrenched power, but also uninhibited fast break vs. tight ball control, foreigners vs. homegrown and, for those who seek significance in such face-offs, even black vs. white."

Howard won, 3–2, and after the game the Bison players ran a victory lap around the field in front of 5,800 fans. A team manager took a telephone off a shelf and handed it to Phillips. "It's President Nixon for you," the manager said. "What have I got to say, Mr. President?" Phillips said into the phone. "Only that I'm disappointed you didn't call sooner." Then he slammed the receiver back on its cradle and laughed, letting the nearby reporters know they were joking. Ian Bain, a

Howard midfielder from Trinidad, told one of those reporters, "This was a victory for our people, Black people."

Not long after Howard's pioneering victory, the NCAA claimed it received letters questioning the eligibility of some of the Bison players. An investigation was launched. Soccer has "always been a game dominated by white Europeans, and the local schools are a little jealous," Phillips told *Ebony* at the time, adding, "It seemed white foreigners were all right . . . black foreigners weren't." Phillips had a point. College teams around the country were using European-born players—the nearby University of Maryland had a team stocked with them—but almost all of those imports were white.

Howard returned to the 1972 NCAA tournament with the investigation still ongoing. Before a semifinals rematch with St. Louis University, the NCAA alerted Howard's athletic director that even if the Bison won, the use of potentially ineligible players meant the team might later have to vacate the win. Phillips was told to sit four players whose eligibility was in question, and the Bison lost. "The NCAA took this game away from us. But that's to be expected. It's pretty evident that a black school is not supposed to win," Phillips said after the game.

Not long after those remarks, the NCAA ruled that from 1970 to 1972 Howard had used ineligible players. Howard was stripped of its 1971 championship and banned from playing in the postseason in 1973. The rules the NCAA claimed Howard had violated pertained to athletes finishing their eligibility in five years, the number of years foreign athletes were permitted to play in their native country before coming to college in the U.S., and the number of scholarship athletes below a certain SAT/ACT score.

Howard president James Cheek declared that it was the Blackness of the foreign athletes that the NCAA (and its member schools) truly objected to. "This discrimination in the present instance is heightened by the fact that the student athletes in question are natives of Black Nations." Phillips put it more succinctly: "Our big mistake was to win the NCAA soccer title."

In his paper about what happened to the Howard soccer team in the early 1970s, Jermaine Scott, a professor at Florida Atlantic University, wrote that the Bison's breakthrough national championship win threatened the establishment in several ways. Primarily, a group of Black players (and a Black coach) from several nations came together, a united minority going up against the "coloniality of sport," a concept that "centers modern sport as a cultural accomplice of the nation-state that reproduces racial hierarchies of white superiority."

For many white families, soccer was a haven for their children. Imagine the shock that Howard's victory in 1971 sent through soccer in America. Scott cites a *U.S. News & World Report* article, which surmised that the "possible reason for the growth of soccer in some suburbs—one that the game's proponents do not discuss publicly, but a few say privately—is that some white youths and their parents want a sport not as dominated by blacks as football and basketball."

Then Howard went out and defeated the all-American white boys from St. Louis University, invading that haven.

It would be incorrect to say that what happened at Howard dissuaded generations of Black families from trying soccer. It was not a tipping point; if anything, it was further affirmation of the existing state of affairs for Black people in the United States. But just as "The American Way" was settling in, as soccer was becoming more suburban and white with each passing year, just as elite club soccer was about to begin its takeover of the sport, a group of Black players and a Black coach came along and proved they were the best. Rather than celebrate that, rather than allow it to inspire young Black athletes around the country, the people who controlled college soccer found a way to delegitimize their accomplishment.

"Take off your shoes."

It was summer 1991, and Kab Hakim, a 24-year-old from Liverpool, England, was standing before twenty kids on an outdoor basketball court at the Takoma Rec Center in northeast Washington, D.C. The court had seen better days. The concrete was cracked and the painted lines were barely visible. The basketball hoops were held up by twin metal bars spaced a couple feet apart; there was no money in the District of Columbia's Department of Parks and Recreation (DPR) budget for the safer, single-gooseneck supports.

"You don't need shoes," Hakim continued. "Don't believe in the shoes. Don't believe in any equipment other than what God's given you, and that's your bare feet."

Hakim stood six-foot-two, with an athletic build. He had long, black curly hair that he kept in a ponytail. His mother was American, but of Scottish and Pakistani descent; the father he never knew was born in India. His ethnicity was a mystery to many of the kids: He wasn't Black like the sixteen boys and four girls seated before him on the court, but he wasn't white either. His thick British accent made him unmistakably not from this place.

The kids, who were between the ages of four and six, did as they were instructed. Puzzled looks on their faces, they slipped off their sneakers. Then Hakim started talking about Brazil. Some of the kids were too young to pick Brazil out on a map, but Hakim lectured them about the country's rich soccer history, about Pelé and Romário and Zico. Brazil produced the best, most creative players in the world, Hakim said, and those great players were once children like them, children from the streets. "Soccer in Brazil is played by kids who can't afford shoes. So that's how you are going to play."

As the kids walked out on the court and split into teams of five, Hakim rolled out a soccer ball and told them he wouldn't be instructing them beyond this: "Do whatever you want to do to beat a player. We're not teaching you any moves; we're not teaching you any tricks. You figure it out with your brain."

Hakim had moved to the United States in 1988. He tried to join the Howard University men's soccer team but wasn't eligible because he'd been paid to play while in England; thus he was no longer an amateur. The university asked if he'd be willing to coach a newly formed women's team. "I'd never seen a girl kick a ball before in my life," he says. "In England, we're very sexist, so girls just didn't play back then. So even though I never saw a girl kick a ball before, I started a women's program." It was the first women's program at a historically Black college, and Hakim coached it for two years. He then became an assistant coach with the men's program, under head coach Keith Tucker.

Hakim and Tucker often discussed ways to find more talented Black players to fill Howard's two teams. The big suburban clubs in Maryland and Virginia were that same "leche with a tinge of café," mostly white but sometimes with one or two Latino or Black kids.

"It just stood to reason that, hey, Howard being in the heart of D.C., you've got to go into the inner city and provide low-income kids with access to the game," Hakim says.

So, in 1991, Hakim helped organize a free ten-week program through DPR that welcomed about eighty kids, mostly from the neighborhood surrounding the Takoma Rec Center. The vast majority of those kids had never touched a soccer ball before. "For most of them it was just free babysitting," Hakim says. "Parents would drop a kid off from eight A.M. and we'd look after them until five P.M." But from those eighty, Hakim identified twenty kids who had some athletic ability and semblance of control over the ball. A few had played soccer before, such as Keith Tucker Jr., the son of the Howard coach, and Alex and Angel Ughiovhe, a brother and sister whose parents had immigrated from Nigeria. But even the kids familiar with the game were so young—the oldest was six—that their exposure to real training had been limited.

For ten weeks that summer, those twenty kids spent much of their days on the basketball court, playing soccer barefoot or in their socks. The space between the hoops' metal poles served as the goals. During breaks, they played foursquare soccer, a version of the playground game but using your feet instead of your hands. True to his word, Hakim barely instructed the kids. He sat back and watched as they figured the game out, trying new ways to beat one another off the dribble, inspired by what they'd seen others try or just making stuff up. By the end of that summer, the four- to six-year-olds had the beginnings of what could be called ball mastery. And then they came back in 1992 and 1993 and 1994, summer after summer, until they reached middle school.

"In the rest of the world, kids aren't coming to an hour practice, two-hour practice, two times a week. It's seven days a week from sunrise to sunset and beyond," Hakim says. "And in places like Brazil they weren't just playing at their own age groups. The ages were mixed. It's a village environment, and that's what we were creating, a village amongst these kids with their bare feet, playing what we called Brazilian soccer."

Today, what Hakim called "Brazilian soccer" is known as futsal, typically a five-on-five game played on a hard surface about the size of a basketball court. Twelve years after Hakim brought those kids together at the Takoma Rec Center, U.S. Soccer would add futsal to the curriculum for U-14 clubs in the Development Academy, its large league of elite club teams, and it has become a standard development tool, particularly in the winter, for top youth clubs and academies (though they play in shoes). But back in 1991, what Hakim was doing would have been seen as radical, if anyone had been paying attention.

He was also unknowingly conducting an experiment of

sorts, bringing a different kind of training to a set of kids typically ignored by America's development system. Hakim's motive back then was clear: Develop some players for Howard University. He didn't know the scope of the issues plaguing soccer in the United States, how "The American Way" had moved the sport into the suburbs. How Pay-to-Play priced out many players. How local and state associations protected the big clubs. And how the top levels of soccer were all but off-limits to Latino and Black players unable or unwilling to endure a hurtful assimilation. While the Latino community had responded by setting up its own clubs and leagues—a sort of separate (but unequal) soccer system— Black people in America mostly gave up on the sport. Parents directed their children to football and basketball, and soccer never really took hold in America's inner cities.

"When I came here, there wasn't really the internet and, other than *Soccer America* maybe, no one was writing about these things," Hakim says. To some degree, he also still held a romanticized idea of what America was, created when he would come to the States as a child in the 1970s, visiting his mom's side of the family up and down the East Coast. He would walk past parks in the evenings and see fields lit up. "The only time I had seen floodlit soccer before was in the stadium. Our parks [in Liverpool], we didn't have lights. We played on the street and in the park, and when it got dark you got to stop. Here, I saw grown men and kids playing pickup soccer under lights. . . . I always thought all Americans were rich, and I was like, 'Wow, one day I would love to come here and play with all these rich people, because they play at night.'"

But after living in D.C. for a few years and interacting with the kids at the Takoma Rec Center, he came to understand that two worlds existed in the U.S., just as they did back in England. "I saw all these poor kids, and I was like, 'These kids are just like me.' Maybe with a different accent. But they're just like me." The community wasn't necessarily big enough to form teams of kids in the same age group, so Hakim was aiming for something different than many youth soccer programs. "They had to be a family," he said. "They had to be a village."

With each passing year, the twenty young players he gathered at the Takoma Rec Center got better and better. Sometimes in the fall or spring, they would come together to play in a local tournament or rec league, and they typically dominated opponents—despite using younger players, despite putting girls on the field with boys. There was not enough funding to continue with other groups below that one, stacking twenty or so talented kids at every age group in a pipeline. So this group was (mostly) a one-off.

When the oldest players got to middle school, Hakim and Tucker and those helping with the program realized that, like it or not, the best players among the twenty needed to join one of the big suburban clubs. There was some thought given to trying to keep them together, augmenting the original group and building out a club team, but that takes money—for travel, for uniforms, for other incidentals— "and you have to remember that this is D.C., where there aren't enough fields, where the fields don't have lights. You are lucky if you are getting an hour a week," Hakim says. The home field the twenty kids played on in rec leagues had a dirt patch in the middle that would get bigger and bigger as the season wore on; eventually the only grass could be found on the outermost edges of the pitch. "And there would always be something random on the field we'd have to report to the ref," Keith Jr. recalls. "One time it was a condom."

For the kids to be seen by college coaches and other influencers, for them to be able to get into the U.S. Youth Soccer Olympic Development Program, they had to be part of the traditional pipeline. There was no other way back then. Although Keith Jr. joined a club whose coach already knew him from school, "for some of the other players, it got toxic," he said of the club environment.

Many of the twenty were told by their club and then high school coaches that they needed to stop "showboating," that the moves they'd honed playing "Brazilian soccer" were hurting the team. "I would hear from other players about things, like how they were limiting their expression," Keith Jr. says. "And maybe some of that was important to learn, but the way it was explained was that to get to the next level they had to not do certain things."

"We would see these other coaches coach our kids, and they're just killing their natural instinct to be creative," Hakim says. "They're getting them to kick the ball long and lay the ball off and just play it simple. It was like, 'You've got average players who can do that. You've got lots of Michael Bradleys. You don't need these kids to be that. You need these kids to be Messi, Ronaldinho, Neymar.'"

When the kids were in high school, Hakim did some fundraising and arranged for some of the boys to come together again. He took them to Europe, where they played the academy teams for Chelsea and West Ham. The team as a collective was not as good as the academy squads, but "individually, we were all the same level in terms of skill," Keith Jr. says. "And no one over there was saying what we were doing was showboating."

Of the original twenty kids, eighteen would play varsity college soccer and one would play college basketball. Alex Ughiovhe was drafted by the Chicago Fire and played in the second division of the United Soccer League. Angel Ughiovhe played in the semi-pro USL W-League, the highest level of women's soccer in the U.S. at the time.

None of the twenty ended up being America's Messi or Neymar or another Mia Hamm, but that's the wrong way of looking at the outcome of the experiment conducted on that basketball court in northeast D.C. To place eighteen of twenty kids on college soccer teams is an extraordinary hit rate. One study of academy participants for England's Premier League teams found that, of the boys who entered the league's academies at age nine, only 0.5 percent eventually made a living playing the game.

"These kids, it was like the movie *Trading Places* but with soccer," Hakim says. "In the movie, they took a homeless guy and showed him the ropes in finance, and you saw him succeed because it wasn't about having money or someone's background or place in life. We gave these kids the ball and put people around them who nurtured them, and look what happened."

Soccer's move into the suburbs during the forming of "The American Way" meant that soccer— unlike, say, football and basketball—never became woven into the fabric of most Black communities. Then the rise of the big clubs and Pay-to-Play made investing in those communities bad for the bottom line. Why would big suburban clubs look elsewhere for players when they already had a steady stream of (mostly) suburban kids from families that could pay the full cost of participation? The few kids from places like northeast D.C. who might have somehow been introduced to the game, who had an interest that could have been cultivated, faced the same financial and cultural issues as Latino players in San Diego (and elsewhere). But in some ways they were even worse off. They didn't have separate clubs and a "Mexican League" to escape to, and they didn't have role models—in, say, the Mexican professional leagues or on the Mexican national team—to look up to, to help them see what was achievable.

"That is really an underrated contributor to the problem, the lack of role models," says Patrick Rose, who grew up outside Baltimore and played for big youth clubs in Baltimore and near D.C.—some years the only Black player on his team—and then at Howard. In 2020, Rose, then an MBA candidate at the Massachusetts Institute of Technology, authored a paper about Black soccer participation. "[Black] kids also just don't see the economic payout in soccer, not the way they can see it with the NBA or NFL," he says.

The on-the-field impact of the exclusion of Black players from the U.S. development pipeline has been devastating. Every conversation around improving the quality of male players includes an emphasis on just getting more kids to play, deepening the talent pool.

Hakim and others see another consequence, one that dovetails a bit with a barstool hypothesis about why the USMNT struggles. It goes: *The U.S. isn't a world power in soccer because its best male athletes play other sports.* This line of thinking ignores too much—coaching, for one—that goes into developing a soccer player, and it presupposes that LeBron James or Patrick Mahomes or Mike Trout would be as good at soccer as they are at their sports. But if the wording of that theory is tweaked a bit, it gets to the heart of what Hakim believes: *The U.S. isn't a world power in soccer because its most "desperate" male athletes play other sports.*

Hakim spent four years living in the Netherlands, and his understanding of player development was influenced by what he saw Ajax do in the late 1970s, and again in the late 1980s. The club twice developed a golden generation of Dutch players.

"First it was [Dennis] Bergkamp, [Marco] van Basten, Bryan Roy, [Frank] Rijkaard, and the core of that group came from inner-city Amsterdam. These were not middle-class kids. Then came another group, and many of them are coming from poverty also," Hakim says. The second group, which emerged around the time Hakim was setting up his program at the Takoma Rec Center, included several Black players—Clarence Seedorf, Edgar Davids, Winston Bogarde, Michael Reiziger, and Patrick Kluivert—who would go on to play for some of the world's biggest clubs.

In excluding Black and Latino players from underserved communities, Hakim believes that the U.S. has kept its pool of talent shallow—and excluded the kids whose drive would lift them (and soccer in the U.S. as a whole) to a higher level.

"Some of the [twenty players] we started with, there was suffering in their lives that you can't escape from. Their friends were getting shot. Their friends were getting arrested. They lived in a suffering environment and they suffered from the day they were born." Hakim says. "Soccer was the escape. That is my point about desperation. Most of the kids playing soccer in America, maybe they work and suffer in the classroom, but when they come home they've got a nice meal and they've got Netflix and a private skills coach and all that. These kids, most of them didn't even have a quarter to go to 7-Eleven. I'm buying them food. I'm buying them drinks. These kids are suffering on a daily basis and whatever relief, whatever escape you can give them, they're loving it."

Patrick Rose now works for one of the handful of organizations trying to bring soccer to those communities. For the most part, the entities that have had success have operated independently of the U.S. Soccer Federation. DC SCORES got its start bringing soccer into area schools in 1999, and by 2021 was serving more than 3,000 kids in sixty schools. It has expanded into thirteen other North American cities. Soccer Starts in the Street was founded in Atlanta in 1989, and by the mid-1990s was in fifty cities, bringing soccer into public housing. There are also a handful of youth clubs trying to bring elite club soccer to underserved communities: Future Soccer Club in D.C., FC Harlem in New York, Spartan Wolves FC in Inglewood, California, and others. "There are great coaches at those clubs who are invested in the game and the kids, but they are strapped for resources," Rose says.

In his MIT paper, Rose listed what it would take for soccer to *really* take hold in Black communities: "Substantial investment and alignment will be needed from corporate sponsors, financiers, the U.S. Soccer Federation, U.S. Soccer Foundation, MLS, state soccer associations, public schools, state and local government, and Historically Black Colleges and Universities (HBCUs). Along with the financial investment, decision-makers have to start caring deeply about the well-being and potential of the Black soccer community in America. . . . Above all, accountability is needed. Leaders need to be held accountable for the low levels of Black soccer participation."

The likelihood of all that happening?

"Yeah, it is a lot," Rose says.

Hakim sees improvement on the margins. Some kids, like those he helped at the Takoma Rec Center, are getting into the game, but until America fully embraces children from those areas, really invests in them as Hakim once did, its potential to produce top players will be constrained.

"America loves to follow trends," he says. "[With soccer] it's tried to follow England, Germany, Spain, etc. They keep copying everybody else. But they don't look within and say, 'What makes our own sports, like basketball and football, so brilliant?' It's because you're developing kids from pure nothing, from poverty, and they're desperate to become the best. That is what it is like with soccer in the rest of the world. But in America, it just isn't there."

SEARCHING FOR MAGGIES

What women's teams have gotten right

It is the obvious question.

Why has the United States been so good at developing female soccer players, feeding teams that have won four World Cup titles and four Olympic gold medals, while simultaneously being so poor at developing male players?

To begin to get at the answer, go back to March 1979, to Chapel Hill, North Carolina. The athletic director at the University of North Carolina, Bill Cobey, called the coach of UNC's men's soccer team, Anson Dorrance, and asked if he'd be willing to evaluate the players on the UNC women's club team as they scrimmaged. At the time, Dorrance was twenty-eight years old and entering his third year coaching the men's team, a part-time employee making $2,500 a season.

What Cobey didn't tell Dorrance was that two days earlier

he'd met with Laura Brockington, a student who had founded the women's club team, which had begun competing only a year earlier. Brockington wanted UNC to have a varsity women's soccer team, and she had been researching which colleges had teams or were planning on starting them. She took her findings to Cobey and, as described in Tim Crothers's excellent biography of Dorrance, *The Man Watching*, she casually mentioned to Cobey that she'd spoken to an attorney who was looking for a Title IX case—referring to the 1972 law that mandated equal treatment for female athletes at federally funded universities.

Cobey had previously been the athletic department's Title IX officer, and for years had pushed UNC to add women's varsity sports. "What clicked in my mind was that maybe this is a time when we can get out ahead of everybody else and we can establish a tradition," Cobey told Crothers. "I knew there was only a handful of women's soccer programs in the nation, and that we had a lot of potential to build something special here."

Cobey had Dorrance evaluate the players, and the coach of the men's team was impressed with their organization and play. A week later, Cobey called Dorrance and made him a full-time employee, now the coach of both the men's and women's varsity teams.

Dorrance would eventually give up coaching the men's team so he could focus solely on women's soccer. He would lead the UNC women's team to twenty-one NCAA titles (out of thirty-one staged, as of 2021). In 1986, he was named the first full-time coach of the USWNT, and he led the U.S. to the title in the inaugural Women's World Cup in 1991.

Women's soccer was not born in Chapel Hill, but the creation of the UNC women's varsity program by Dorrance was effectively the birth of a new pathway for female players in America, one that would spread to other universities around the country. Together those schools would become the most formidable development system for female players in the world.

So how did the creation of one varsity program at UNC lead to all of that?

Start with Dorrance. He was born in India in 1951 and had lived in Kenya, Ethiopia, Malaysia, and Belgium. His father was an American oil executive, so most of his childhood was spent abroad, with trips home to work on his grandparents' farm in North Carolina. His mother, Peggy, was the best athlete in the family; she played tennis and had been on the swim team at American University in Washington, D.C. Maggie, Anson's older sister, was the best athlete among the kids. In *The Man Watching*, Crothers writes of an incident where Anson came home bragging about winning a school boxing tournament. Maggie promptly put on some gloves and knocked one of Anson's teeth out. Peggy and Maggie's influence, the fact that they were superior athletes and also highly competitive, shaped Dorrance's view of female athletes. The best athletes he knew growing up were women, and they were tough—fighters, winners at all costs. "And growing up, I didn't have the influences, such as American television, that taught you that men were supposed to be more dominant athletes," Dorrance says.

When he began building the UNC women's program in the early 1980s, he described the atmosphere around soccer (and all sports in America): "If a male is competitive, everyone puts him on a pedestal. If a girl is competitive, she gets rejected, even by her own gender." He didn't subscribe to that thinking, and as he worked to stock his roster in the early years of the program, he went searching for young women like his sister, a team of Maggies willing to put on the gloves and knock your teeth out in order to prove they were better. He looked less for soccer talent—some of his first recruits had barely played the sport—and more for a certain spirit.

The first few UNC women's teams were filled with hard-charging, hard-partying, confident women. Some of them were openly gay, at least among their teammates. "We let them be who they were. We didn't condescend in training. We went after it. And the ones that had that competitive spirit, we let it come out," Dorrance says. "One of my favorite comments was from Mia Hamm, who said that when she [came to UNC in 1989]: 'I could finally be who I wanted to be.'"

Early on, Dorrance's coaching philosophy was to coach women the same way he coached men. That was tidy. It sounded good. But his thinking evolved, and as UNC became the nation's most dominant program, he gave speeches and shared his philosophy on the differences between coaching men and women. One example he has often cited is his approach to offering praise. If he praised a male player in public, telling the entire team how that player had carried the team, the other male players nodded in agreement. Do the same with a female player in front of the entire team and, in Dorrance's experience, every woman in the room now hates that player—and the player being praised now hates the coach for putting her in that position. Dorrance began praising his female players in private, because his belief was that what female players cared about most was knowing that *he* saw their brilliance.

Dorrance's views on coaching the different genders are, then and now, controversial, and the finer points of his approach can be debated. But in the context of the rise of women's soccer in the United States, how the country became the best in the world at producing female players, what stands out most is the kind of players he recruited and what he demanded of them.

Stories about the intensity of Dorrance's training sessions are legendary. He talked to players about "the gift of fury," for example, and may be best known in coaching circles for "the competitive cauldron," his system of creating competition in training by using fitness testing and data collection. UNC players were ranked in twenty-four different categories (effort, passing, IVI, etc.), and a scoresheet was posted, with players moving up and down during the season. It meant that every moment of every training session mattered. Take a day off and your score would suffer. Soon you might find yourself at the bottom of the list . . . a loser. Early in the preseason, Dorrance would stage a scrimmage of starters vs. freshmen and returning reserves, and in those games the coaching staff deliberately swallowed their whistles. Elbows were thrown into freshman faces; they were picked up and thrown down; studs were up on tackles. *Welcome to the UNC way, freshmen.*

Crothers listed some of the nicknames Dorrance had for

his players over the years: Buzzsaw, Hammer, Wild Thing, Yellow Card, Angry Chicken, Tiny Terminator. He wanted his players to be "killers."

In Chapel Hill, Dorrance did not just build a program unlike any other in college soccer. He built something that didn't exist anywhere else in the world. It was, ostensibly, the first women's professional academy. Yes, the players were in college and went to class. Yes, they were unpaid, bound by NCAA rules, technically "amateurs." But in terms of the quality of the players brought in—basically a handful of the top eighteen-year-olds each year—and the quality of the coaching, the level of commitment, and the standard of performance demanded of the players, this was a professional setup. Starting in the early 1980s, when almost every top high school player in the country ended up at UNC, the U.S. had the best finishing school for young female players in the world. No other country had anything close, and that meant that the U.S. talent pool, with each passing year, got deeper and better, and the gap between the U.S. and other countries grew wider and wider.

At the same time, a "tidal wave was happening," Dorrance says. That wave was the realization by universities across the U.S. that adding women's soccer could help them comply with Title IX. There was no cap on the roster size for women's soccer, meaning schools could add thirty-plus female athletes to their rolls. Furthermore, many of the colleges looking to start a women's varsity program already had a men's program, so practice fields and a place to play games were already in place. It was a cost-effective way to comply with the law. These new programs sometimes hired former

UNC players, and those coaches and others modeled their programs on what Dorrance had built in Chapel Hill. UNC became the shining example of what could be, and programs around the country were built using its blueprint. In 1972, the year Title IX was passed, only two colleges offered scholarships for women's soccer. Today, there are more than 330 at the Division I level alone.

"What you see now at the youth level, with all this scholarship money out there and the opportunities to win college scholarships, is so many good clubs and so many good players," Dorrance says. "We are all riding this wave."

There is something else you now see at the youth level, something that Dorrance likes to talk about more than anything else when it comes to discussing his influence on the women's game. Sitting in the upstairs office of his home in North Carolina, Dorrance, now seventy-one and still coaching UNC, will engage on any issue from his thirty-five years coaching women's soccer. But what he most loves talking about is his belief that the advantage the U.S. women have over other countries is mostly about will, about the spirit he mined for as he crossed the country each year looking for Maggies to fill his roster, and the way he enhanced that spirit in his players.

To make this point, he tells a story: One night he was watching Rachel Maddow on MSNBC and she introduced a guest as an "expert." The guest surprisingly turned that assertion—that he was an "expert"—back on Maddow. "What are *you* an expert in?" he asked Maddow. "And she had the perfect answer," Dorrance says. "She said, 'I am an expert in reading comprehension.' I really like that answer.

And as I thought about it, it made me think a lot about *What am I an expert in?* And it was very refreshing for me to sort out what separated me from other coaches. What I concluded was that I, Anson Dorrance, am an expert in competition. Other people know more about the game than I do. What sets me apart is I am an expert in competing."

When Dorrance was appointed the U.S. women's national team coach in 1986, the team had never won a game in international competition. Five years later, they were world champions. "I didn't go out there and play the way the world was playing. I took elements of the American spirit and I coached through that spirit," Dorrance says. "I know how to compete, to train my athletes to compete, and to inspire them to compete versus their opponents. That's what I brought to the U.S. women's national team. For eight years I baked in this competitive fire."

Dorrance dropped the 4-4-2 formation most countries favored and put in a 4-3-3 that smothered teams with high pressure. He did that at UNC and then with the USWNT. He recruited and trained players who flew into tackles, who competed to the point of exhaustion, who displayed athleticism and skill, sure, but who also had bite. What he baked into the culture of women's soccer in America was the idea that it was more than all right to be a killer; it was a prerequisite for being great.

In countries such as Germany, there is a consistency to what is taught to boys at the youth level on up through the professional ranks and the German men's national team. There is not complete uniformity, of course, but what could be called "The German Way" of training and playing exists throughout the system. Dorrance created the same for women's soccer in the United States. Go to any major girls' soccer tournament today—especially one involving teams from the Elite Clubs National League—and you'll see team after team playing the high-pressing 4-3-3 formation that Dorrance championed. And you'll see young girls throwing elbows and flying into tackles. There is great athleticism, of course, and elite technical ability, but what you notice most is that there are Maggies all over the field. The spirit, the bite that Dorrance fostered in his players, is the prevailing standard.

"There are these galvanizing elements that make [Americans] special," Dorrance says. "We are cowboys. We love duels. Our whole platform is you beat a player off the dribble and you stop a player on the dribble. You win in the air offensively and defensively. You combine that aggressive style with athleticism and skill. That's who we are."

But back to the original question: Why has the United States been so good at developing female soccer players and so poor at developing male players?

The U.S. was first to really embrace and invest in the women's game, because of Title IX. It had a hub of innovation in Chapel Hill and, in Dorrance, a thought leader willing to share his secret sauce and push the game in different directions. Over the years, the character traits of a top U.S. player were clearly defined, and how female teams should play was modeled. This can now be seen from the top to the bottom of the development pyramid.

That last point, the creation of a distinctly American type of player and style of play—call it "The Cowboy Way"—shouldn't be undersold. It has been one of the biggest flaws in the development system for male players in America. At the youngest levels, boys' soccer is a hodgepodge of styles, every coach or club finding its own identity. It is the same in men's collegiate soccer and Major League Soccer. The U.S. Men's National Team has for much of the past three decades found the most success setting up to defend and counter— that is, sitting back and absorbing the blows of an opponent and hoping to catch them off-balance. No one would mistake that for "The Cowboy Way." That may have been out of necessity; the USMNT lacked the skillful attacking talents to play differently against elite opponents. But it was also the byproduct of a disorganized and disparate system. The U.S. women had a tight development pyramid, starting with Dorrance at the top and everyone lining up perfectly below him. On the men's side, there was no such figure, no such leadership. There was no pyramid at all, really, just a bunch of stones scattered about.

Around 2004, the French professional men's team Olympique Lyonnais approached a local women's club team—FC Lyon— and essentially merged that group into its operation, connecting it to one of France's largest professional clubs. The development was not unlike what happened at UNC in the late 1970s. An organization with a men's team decided to get into women's soccer, so it took an existing women's team in the area and bestowed on it a different status. That it happened almost twenty-five years later in France tells you how much of a head start the United States had in the women's game.

The early seasons of Olympique Lyonnais Féminin mirrored Anson Dorrance's first few years coaching the UNC women in several ways—most notably in how bare-bones the operation was. The Lyon women were not treated as equal to the men; the Lyon players initially didn't have proper training gear or even the same uniforms as the men's side. In the semifinals of the 2004 women's Champions League, Lyon played Arsenal on a rainy day in England. At halftime, Lyon president Jean-Michel Aulas was wringing out the jerseys of his players, and it occurred to him that, had this been the men's team, the players would have simply changed into their second set of uniforms. Aulas would later tell Reuters that it was at that moment that he vowed to bring equality to the setup at Lyon, to create an environment where the men's and women's teams were treated the same. That would not extend to compensation—the women are still paid far less than Lyon's men, which is true in the U.S. as well—but in terms of facilities and support staff, Aulas got it close.

Since 2004, Lyon has won seven Champions League titles; from 2016 to 2020 it won five in a row. What UNC was to women's collegiate soccer in the U.S., Lyon became to professional soccer in Europe. Aulas recruited the best players from around the world; the 2021 Lyon squad featured players from ten different countries. That included Ada Hegerberg, the 2018 recipient of the Ballon d'Or Féminin, given to the best female player in the world. In previous years, Aulas recruited U.S. stars Megan Rapinoe and Alex Morgan to Lyon. While the best teenage American players have long dreamed of going to UNC, the best in Europe started dreaming of one day playing for Lyon.

Other European professional clubs followed Lyon's lead,

prioritizing the women's game for the first time, just as many U.S. colleges had copied UNC decades earlier. In the past few years, many of the continent's biggest clubs (Chelsea, Manchester United, Paris Saint-Germain, Barcelona) have invested in their women's teams like never before. Without a law such as Title IX, it is left to the clubs to decide what is equal—or equal enough—in terms of facilities, staff, etc., and pay inequity remains a persistent problem. Some clubs have had to be publicly shamed into treating their women's team more like their men's side. But there is no question that women's professional soccer is booming in Europe, and that has raised the level of performance across the world as the best female players head there, and to the U.S.-based National Women's Soccer League (NWSL), to play.

Aulas didn't stop with his senior team. In 2013, Lyon created a youth academy, and the club vowed to build a development pipeline similar to what existed on the men's side. French male stars Karim Benzema, Alexandre Lacazette, and others were developed by Lyon from a young age; Benzema drew the attention of the club's scouts in a U-10 match. Aulas hired a staff to mine for similar female talent, and within a few years a third of the women's senior team came out of the academy. Gradually, clubs across Europe built their own academies, and suddenly some of Europe's biggest teams were boasting about the talented young female players coming out of their pipeline. In 2021, Barcelona allowed nine girls to move into its famed La Masia men's training center. The setup that had produced Lionel Messi, Xavi, Andrés Iniesta, and other La Liga stars was now integrated.

What Lyon built and how it trickled down to other clubs

also raised the level of play of national teams across Europe. You didn't have to look hard or have a keen understanding of the game to see it. Between the 2015 and 2019 World Cups, the chasm between the U.S. women and most of the rest of the world narrowed significantly.

In 2019, "at the World Cup, technically, France was just as good. The Germans, the Dutch, England, tactically they were just as good," Dorrance says. "And you could see with other teams, such as Spain and Italy, when you watch them play, if they had a goal scorer, they could have gone to the final. They were just missing that piece that could consistently score, a Hamm, a [Michelle] Akers, an [Abby] Wambach."

From Chapel Hill, Dorrance observed the World Cup and later watched as the USWNT lost to Sweden in its opening game of the 2020 Summer Olympics and then was knocked out by Canada in the semifinals. For decades, the U.S. had the only real development system for elite female players in the world. Now development systems were popping up at professional clubs across Europe, and more and more players were getting top coaching and competing against elite players every day. The impact had been transformative.

Dorrance is still bullish on the U.S. maintaining its perch atop world soccer. There is that mentality, "The Cowboy Way," that Dorrance helped ingrain in the system, and the sheer number of girls playing soccer in the U.S. still dwarfs that of any other country. But he acknowledges that women's soccer in America is at an inflection point. If teams in Europe are building professionalized pathways for young female players, if more and more begin taking the development of girls seriously, as Lyon and other clubs have done, how long before what is offered at UNC and other U.S. colleges becomes something significantly lesser?

We may already be at that point. The NCAA places limits on practice hours; players must attend classes, meet certain academic standards. At Lyon, young female players visit with psychologists, and some participate in hypnosis sessions and yoga. How many American colleges offer their players that? United States colleges have arranged visits to Lyon to tour its facilities and probe its methods, but some things you can't replicate. "When you're 16 in Europe, you can play for your pro team. You can go train with women who are 10 years older. That's an accelerated development that we can't re-create here," Kate Markgraf, the general manager of the USWNT, told *Soccer America* in 2019.

In 2020, the parent company of Olympique Lyonnais bought the NWSL's OL Reign, based in Tacoma, Washington. That partnership could mirror what is happening with some Major League Soccer and United Soccer League teams, with a big European club getting a foothold in the States to better mine for young talent. "That is basically Lyon planting their flag in Tacoma," Dorrance says. "They are clever. I want to see what comes of that."

In the summer of 2021, Lyon's senior team traveled to Portland, Oregon, to play in the Women's International Champions Cup. Barcelona and two NWSL teams, the Houston Dash and host Portland Thorns, filled out the event. The Thorns and Lyon met in the final in August at Providence Park, and among the starters that evening for the Thorns was fifteen-year-old Olivia Moultrie. She was born in Southern California and at age eleven visited Chapel Hill. She was so special that Dorrance took her commitment to play for UNC even though it would be about eight years before she would be old enough to enroll.

Two years later, Moultrie's plans changed. In 2018, she visited Lyon, Paris Saint-Germain, and Bayern Munich in Germany. She and her parents began investigating pathways that didn't involve a stop in college. Eventually she signed an endorsement deal with Nike and began training with the Thorns, even though an NWSL rule prohibited her from signing a professional contract with the club.

"I feel for literally almost every kid in girls' soccer, you should go to college; there's not a million dollars at the end of the rainbow," her father, K. C. Moultrie, told *The New York Times*. "I think if you're truly, truly elite, if your goal is to be a world-class player and a pro and, in Olivia's case, to be the best player in the world, there's no way it's better to play college than it is to play full time."

In 2021, Moultrie challenged the NWSL's rule that a player had to be eighteen to sign a professional contract with one of the league's teams, and a federal judge eventually ruled that the age restriction violated federal antitrust law. Eliminating the rule would also bring gender equity to soccer, the judge wrote in her decision, because there was no such age restriction on male players signing with Major League Soccer.

That August, in the semifinals of the Women's International Champions Cup, Moultrie started her first game for the Thorns and also scored her first professional goal. Then she started the final against Lyon, and the Thorns won, 1–0. It was hard not to find significance in that moment. One of the best young players in America had skipped college and was playing as a professional, against the professional club that has been the leader in pushing women's soccer in Europe to new levels.

Some American girls are likely to forgo college, Dorrance predicts, taking the Moultrie route, either signing with NWSL teams or ones in Europe. But most NWSL teams are far behind Lyon and other European clubs in terms of youth development; they haven't needed to invest in it because the college system did it for them. If NWSL teams don't significantly invest in their academies, it is not unreasonable to expect that the best female teenage players will bolt for Lyon or Barcelona or another club offering a superior development pathway. For decades, a spot at UNC or another elite college program has been the best option for young female players. In the near future, it might be the route of second-tier players, and gradually women's college soccer could look more like it does on the men's side, less and less relevant as a development option with each passing year.

Dorrance doesn't see women's college soccer diminishing to that point. He likens female soccer development to investing, and the U.S. is going to want a "varied stock portfolio," betting on some kids who go to a pro team early, others who end up in college. Much will depend on how Moultrie does, he admits. (The performance of Mallory Pugh, another player who jumped straight from high school to the NWSL, in 2017, has been a mixed bag; she is on her third pro team and didn't make the 2020 Olympic team.) What is irrefutable is that the landscape for women's soccer is changing, and that UNC and Dorrance are no longer the lone guiding light—no longer enough to give the U.S. an edge.

II

In 1995, Matt Carver landed in Germany, stationed in what is now known as United States Army Garrison Bavaria–Hohenfels Training Area. He was a married 23-year-old living fewer than sixty miles from the Czech Republic, once again an Iowa boy in a strange land.

Between his trips to Harlem as a boy and his arrival in Germany, Carver had compiled a string of impressive accomplishments: captain of the Urbandale High School football and soccer teams; student body president; named Best Athlete, Best Attitude, Most Concerned, and Best Smile in his senior yearbook. He gained admission to Notre Dame, his top choice, and joined the ROTC program to pay for college. After earning degrees in government and history and graduating cum laude, he was commissioned as a second lieutenant and would rise to the rank of lieutenant colonel.

Along the way, Carver would find himself in situations that echoed his Harlem experience, moments when the suburban Iowa boy once again engaged with people from vastly different backgrounds. At Notre Dame in 1990, his freshman year roommate, Leroy Greene, was from Wichita, Kansas, and the rare Black student who was not on the football or basketball team. (Carver would wonder later if the pairing had been intentional; he wrote his application essay about his trips to Harlem.) In their shared 9-by-13-foot space in Dillon Hall, Carver heard about how his roommate's mother raised four kids on $12,000 a year; how his father had once been run out of an Oklahoma town he was visiting. When Carver would go to the local mall, store clerks would readily take a check from him if he showed his Notre Dame ID. Those same clerks refused to take a check from his roommate; the Notre Dame ID was insufficient in *his* case.

After Notre Dame, in the army, Carver became part of "just the absolute melting pot," he says, and he gravitated toward those who were more Harlem than Urbandale. One of his early friends there, John Lopez, once pulled up a map on his computer showing where the shootings and murders in Los Angeles had occurred that year. "You see that? See where the highest number is?" Lopez said, pointing to a spot on the map. "That is where I grew up."

In the village of Hörmannsdorf, Carver and his wife, Renee, found a farmhouse to live in that was not far from the Hohenfels Training Area. His landlords learned he liked soccer and introduced him to a few players from the district league club, SV Hörmannsdorf, which had a first and second team. He practiced with them, played a game with the second team, then was pushed up to the first team. He was a young, athletic, industrious left back.

On Sundays, the second team would play, followed by the first team—the marquee game. To Carver, it seemed like every man, woman, and child in Hörmannsdorf would "show up, pay a few deutsche marks for some sausage and beer and so they could yell at the referee and the players."

He loved it.

Carver also enjoyed competing with and against soccer players unlike those he'd faced in Iowa. There was one, a midfielder named Christian Wild, who had climbed a few rungs of German professional football, but he was now in his late twenties, playing for a tiny club in a tiny village, grand dreams dashed but the joy of the game still at his feet. "I couldn't tell you then, still couldn't tell you, whether he was right-footed or left-footed," Carver says. "He wasn't fast enough to play at the highest levels in Germany, but technically I had never seen a player like him." Watching him, Carver recalled the best player he had competed with in high school. That player had landed a college scholarship and played several years for the Minnesota Thunder in the second division of U.S. Soccer, but the German player was technically so much stronger.

Carver's first child, daughter Jessi, was born in his second year in Germany, so it was inevitable that he took note of the local kids playing for SV Hörmannsdorf. He watched them train, saw how organized it all was, and marveled at the youngest kids' skill and passion. At SV Hörmannsdorf, kids paid only 60 euros (or about $70) for a *full year* of soccer. It didn't matter if a player was eight years old or eighteen; they all paid that same nominal amount.

One afternoon, Carver noted how the training setup for the kids' teams included fields with some sort of backstop (a wall or fence or net) behind the goal. He thought back to the wide-open fields he played on in Urbandale and recognized the point of those barriers: No time was wasted chasing balls. It was a simple thing, yes, but contributed to a more efficient training session. Carver would notice these backstops on nearly every soccer field as he and Renee traveled throughout Germany.

There was also something intangible, something he wouldn't put his finger on until later: The cultivation of players, building them up, was hugely important not only to the club but to the town's residents. Even if the result was that one of those young players would get shipped off to a bigger club, the village took great pride in the process that lifted them. "When a child from there was asked to play for a team nearby that was a little bit bigger, everyone was so proud," Carver says. "It was not a competitive thing; it was a positive thing, like everyone had succeeded." In Germany, it might not have taken a village to develop a soccer player, but the village sure acted like it had a big role to play.

In 1998, Carver and his family moved back to the States so he could attend law school at the University of Iowa. After he graduated, they settled in Urbandale, now a family of five. But in 2003 his National Guard unit—he was the commander of the 1088th Personnel Service detachment—was deployed to Kuwait. He was there until 2005, finally coming off active duty in February of that year.

Before the deployment, he'd coached Jessi's team in the Urbandale Soccer Club (USC), the same club Carver had played for as a child. (Like most players of his generation, he started in AYSO but then moved to a club.) With USC, he coached the girls to be aggressive, to press, like Anson Dorrance's "killers." Around Des Moines, girls' soccer was as big as or bigger than boys' soccer, with so many parents and their children chasing the dream of a college scholarship. When he returned from Kuwait in 2005 with his three children (his fourth, Rockne, would be born a year later), now all old enough to play on teams, he threw himself into working with the club even more, wanting to be of service to his community, just as his parents had been.

Around 2007, he joined the USC's board of directors. It had become a different club by then, thanks to an agreement with the neighboring Johnston Soccer Club. The two clubs maintained separate recreational programs but arranged to have their best players—those playing select soccer—come together at the U-11 level and above, on teams under the banner of the Johnston Urbandale Soccer Club (JUSC). "Both clubs weren't having the success they had in the past, and this was a way to make the club bigger and more competitive," Carver says.

If you combined the number of players in the two clubs' recreational programs and the elite players at JUSC, the number of kids was still not comparable to a large club in, say, suburban Philadelphia or Dallas. The combined population of Urbandale and Johnston in 2008 was fewer than 55,000—but in this slice of America, two clubs had essentially become one, and that one was now bigger and more influential.

Remember those backstops in Germany that Carver noticed? One of his first attempts to improve the recreational program at the Urbandale Soccer Club was to explain to the board what he'd seen in Germany and propose that the club do the same for the fields it rented at the Urbandale Soccer Complex. "I ended up doing the research into this, with a fencing company in Des Moines, and got some quotes and went back to the board," Carver says. He was a little sheepish as he offered up the quote for the backstops. "It was going to be like $15,000 or something like that for a couple of them. I was concerned that this kind of expense, it was significant, and how was the club going to afford that?"

The board agreed to pay for it without blinking.

Carver later went to the club treasurer and asked how USC could afford such a large expenditure. How much money did they have on hand? "Enough," the treasurer offered.

"This went on for a while," Carver says. "I would ask him how much money the club had for things, and he would just say, 'Enough.'" Carver persisted; he was a board member and he wanted to know the number.

"Finally, he told me that the club had like $330,000 in an account. My jaw just dropped."

How does a recreational soccer club in suburban Des Moines accumulate a reserve fund in excess of $300,000? And why would it even need that kind of money on hand?

Those questions and others percolated. As a 501(c)(3) nonprofit, the club's financial forms were available online, and Carver pored over them. What he found was not just a club with an incredibly robust reserve fund. He saw a business, and it changed the way he viewed the Urbandale Soccer Club and the Johnston Urbandale Soccer Club and, eventually, youth soccer across the state and across the country.

As Carver began poking around the finances of the local clubs, he saw figures that to him didn't add up. He questioned why the recreational program was charging around $70 per season (or $140 for the year) at the youngest levels when the actual cost of participation—what it cost the club—was, according to his math, around $25 per season. He didn't believe anyone at the club was doing anything improper or for their personal gain, just that this was the way USC had long operated and they wanted to maintain the status quo.

In 2009, amid the Great Recession, USC's board took up a

proposal to raise the salaries of the club's six paid coaches, individuals for whom coaching youth soccer was their primary (or only) job, as opposed to the volunteer parent coaches. The total expenditure for their salaries would rise to about $317,000—a 16 percent bump. Those coaches would now be making, on average, $50,000 a year.

That was not significantly higher than the median salary in Des Moines at the time, but Carver did not like that this raise was coming during a recession, and he questioned whether the hours the coaches were working warranted that level of compensation. During one meeting he told board members, "This is a 501(c)(3), we need to ensure that there's not private inurement occurring here. We may have individuals who are being overcompensated for the work they are doing." He also asked to see a breakdown of the hours the coaches worked.

"They told me, 'Matt, you're micromanaging. They're doing a great job.' I said, 'It's not about whether they're doing a great job or not. It's about, are we overpaying them for that great job they're doing?'"

Carver did the math on his own, and he estimated that the clubs were paying those six coaches approximately $400 an hour. At the law firm Carver had previously worked at, he billed clients $150 an hour.

He also objected to the fact that, to help pay for the coaches' salaries, $40,000 would be drawn from the Urbandale Soccer Club recreational program, when most of the coaches were running elite teams at JUSC. Why was revenue from the recreational program subsidizing coaches for the select teams? Yes, some of those coaches ran clinics and sometimes attended recreational practices, but in Carver's mind what was being provided to the recreational kids was not worth the money being taken from the recreational program.

One can imagine how Carver's scrutiny went over with the other board members and the paid coaches at a club that had been operating this way since the 1990s. He fought club administrators on other issues as well, such as the fact that the JUSC elite teams got access to the best fields multiple times a week, while recreational teams could rarely get time more than once a week. He also angered club officials when he used a registration loophole to position his daughter Jessi's team so it could play at the select level without technically being part of JUSC; that way, his players didn't have to pay the much higher JUSC registration fee.

"I was the squeaky wheel," Carver says.

It was to no one's surprise then, when, in September 2010, Carver resigned from the USC board. In his resignation letter, he wrote: "I am not sure you are all aware of this, but the United States is the only country in the world that has made youth soccer such an expensive 'pay for play' endeavor."

Within the Urbandale soccer community, Carver was likely viewed as just another overzealous parent.

"I think people thought I was just going to take my daughters' two teams and go to another club," he says, in order to keep coaching them and not lose players to the elite team at JUSC, with its paid coaches.

But what would that have fixed?

People who saw it that way surely didn't know that Carver viewed the soccer-playing children of Urbandale and the surrounding areas much like the kids he'd met back in Harlem or the boy in his sixth-grade class who hadn't been chosen for the gifted program.

Not long after he resigned from the USC board, Carver talked with his father. Matt's frustration with how the Urbandale Soccer Club operated had been a frequent topic between the two over the years, but now Matt let Mike Carver know what he was going to do about it: That spring, he would start the J-Hawk Soccer Club, a low-cost playing option for kids in the area, an alternative to USC/JUSC.

"Matthew, what you need to realize is what you're starting is a considerable threat to an establishment," Mike Carver responded. "You are gonna be seen as a threat, and you are gonna be treated as a threat. Be ready."

5

WHEN MESSI STARTED TO WALK

How to introduce the game to children

As the designated start time for his presentation approaches and parents and coaches file in, finding a seat in one of the blue chairs arranged in rows in the front hall of Glenn York Elementary School, Tom Byer begins to move in place just a bit, a slight rocking that could be perceived as nervousness but is really excitement.

Byer, sixty-two, is wearing a black Adidas track shirt with the Houston Dynamo logo on it. He looks very much a part of the Dynamo organization. A few hours earlier, at the team's fan fest, Byer had appeared on the big screen inside BBVA Stadium to promote his appearance at Glenn York Elementary, and he was interviewed about his developmental philosophy: Soccer Starts at Home. Byer played briefly in college and professionally, but he no longer carries himself like an athlete. He spikes his black hair with a little gel but otherwise his look now is that of a dad lounging in a tracksuit on a Sunday morning.

Byer has given this presentation more than a hundred times all around the world. He's been doing it so long now that he could be forgiven for going through the motions, putting it on autopilot. But he's incapable of doing that. No matter the audience or the venue, there is this moment, he says, when people realize that what he is proposing just makes sense. The anticipation of that jazzes him. The confirming nods, the look in people's eyes when they "get it," the videos he receives later of little kids slickly handling a ball, the remarks from parents about how everything changed once they heard him speak: That is his addiction.

Standing before the coaches and parents, moments before he'll go to his computer and start projecting images on a large screen behind him, he knows a wave of validation is coming.

In the back of the room at Glenn York Elementary, Paul Holocher, the Dynamo's academy director since July 2018, leans against a wall. He occasionally glances at his phone while also monitoring who enters the room. He greets a few coaches and parents he knows, gets introduced to others. With some, he points to the front of the room, to Byer, and tells them how much they are going to enjoy his talk. Many of the arriving coaches know that Holocher was hired away from the San Jose Earthquakes to take on the herculean task of bringing some structure to the Houston youth soccer scene. Over in Dallas, local youth clubs are pumping out top prospects, with many matriculating to the FC Dallas academy. The Houston development pathway has been far less organized and fruitful. To get more great players into the Dynamo academy, Holocher must help local coaches rethink their approach to teaching soccer. He can run coaching clinics (as he did an hour earlier on a grass field just outside the school), but that will only do so much. He must also retrain parents, the first coaches in the development pipeline.

To help with that, Holocher and the Dynamo turned to Tom Byer, a somewhat controversial figure in U.S. soccer circles. Byer was born in New York's Hudson Valley, the son of a police officer, but for more than three decades he has lived in Japan, where he made his mark as a technical coach and then as a promoter of Soccer Starts at Home. Some in the United States consider him little more than a pitchman, a self-promoter, lacking the right credentials or experience. This absolutely bothers him; he doesn't try to hide it. He and his ideas have been embraced in other countries and by some of the biggest names in global soccer, yet many of the power brokers in his homeland want nothing to do with him. That is a jagged rock in his shoe that he just can't shake loose.

Much of the early part of Byer's presentation at Glenn York Elementary is spent proving to those in the room that he should be taken seriously. He explains how he went from a nobody to one of Japan's most famous sporting figures; he highlights his many media appearances; he touts the approval he has received from people at the highest levels of the game. Even in private, when you first meet him, he reflexively goes to this material. He's a name-dropper, a tireless supplier of anecdotes about his connections, but he is no braggart. Byer did not have a lustrous college or professional playing career; he never racked up wins coaching at any level. His résumé, using those metrics, is thin, so he's always working against that, perpetually an outsider trying to get people to understand why he's really an insider.

To wit, Byer delivered this string of words about five minutes into our first meeting: "Rio Ferdinand, the captain of Manchester United, flies all the way to China to spend a day with me because he wanted to see my presentation. I show it to him and he sits back in his chair and he goes, 'Mate, is it too late for an eight-year-old? Because I've been doing everything wrong with my son.' These are exact quotes. I'm not making this up. I was invited to Manchester United when I first started out by Ryan Giggs. I got there. I'm having dinner with him, I show him the presentation. His son is the same age as my son who's in all of my videos so he asks me, he goes, 'When are you leaving to go back to London?' I said, 'Blah, blah, blah.' And he said, 'Okay, come to my restaurant tomorrow.' I go to his restaurant and he's got Gary Neville, Phil Neville, Paul Scholes. He brought some of the greatest players to play and I'm showing these guys the presentation. I presented to the head of coach education for the German FA right after they won the World Cup in 2014. He sat right in the front row of my presentation and when I got done he told me to come here and sit down next to him, and he patted me on the back."

Byer got through the star-studded anecdote in what seemed like a single breath.

Eventually, Byer gets to the meat of his presentation, and it involves his two sons: Kaito and Sho. As Byer and his wife, Midori, contemplated how they would introduce the two young boys to soccer, Byer had an epiphany. He took a dozen or so Size 1 soccer balls (often called "mini balls" or "minis") and scattered them around his home. He encouraged the boys to play with them as they moved around, providing little instruction beyond *not* encouraging them to boot the balls. In video clips, you see Kaito and Sho go from slowly moving the ball from foot to foot, looking as clumsy as any young child, to becoming more and more comfortable with the ball at their feet. Their abilities with the ball keep improving, until they're doing pirouettes around the living room, elasticos down the hall, slick move after slick move. When he finally cuts to a video of Kaito in a game in Japan at age ten, weaving around players with his superior ball skills, parents in the room begin nodding, the lesson absorbed. "In terms of ball mastery, they are now way above average for their age," Byer tells the parents.

Byer senses the buy-in—this is *that* moment—and he gets even more excited, talking faster, moving around the room more, a preacher with an enraptured flock.

"Tom is a big part of what we are trying to build here," Holocher says later. Then he adds, "And I don't understand why we are the only ones working with him."

The year was 1983, and Tom Byer, then twenty-three, was holding on to the last threads of a professional playing career. After a brief collegiate career at South Florida, he trained with the Tampa Bay Rowdies of the dying North American Soccer League (NASL), then had a stint with Leiston FC, a low-level club in England. He then landed in Japan, the first American to play there, for Hitachi FC. It would be wrong to paint that move as pioneering. Japan was a soccer outpost, one of the last rungs for a player hanging on to the dream.

After about a year there, Byer retired but stuck around. He found work putting on soccer clinics at schools for expatriate kids and on military bases, places where his limited Japanese wasn't a problem. At one of those clinics in 1989, he met a boy who mentioned that his father worked for Nestlé. About a week later, in need of financing to expand his clinics, he cold-called that boy's home. Luckily, the kid answered. Byer asked to speak to the boy's father, then casually inquired as to what the father's position was at Nestlé. "He's the president," the boy responded. A short time later, Byer had a deal with Nestlé to sponsor fifty clinics that he would stage for Japanese kids around the country, and Nestlé would continue to sponsor him for the next eleven years.

Renée Byer, Tom's older sister and a Pulitzer Prize–winning photographer, went to visit Tom in Tokyo right after he'd signed the deal with Nestlé. She knew he was hustling soccer in Japan; they occasionally talked. Then she arrived and they went out to dinner with a group of Tom's friends. "We were at this restaurant with some people, including this one guy," Renée said. "I can't speak Japanese, but they are trying to explain to me that this one guy is like the Eddie Murphy of Japan. The next day we fly to an island off Japan to do one of [Tom's] clinics, and I get to the hotel and turn on the TV and there is that guy, the Eddie Murphy of Japan, on a sitcom. And that's when I got it. [Tom] had really infiltrated this culture and engaged this country."

As he was putting on the clinics, Byer embraced a developmental philosophy—the Coerver Method—devised by Wiel Coerver, a Dutch coach. Rather than put kids on the field and let their natural ability come through, Coerver believed in teaching specific moves to young players, the feints and pullbacks and such that they would use on the field. He studied the greatest players of all time, cataloged the moves they utilized, and then drilled players on how to do them. Only after kids mastered those moves did they move on to passing and shooting and tactics. Arjen Robben, Cristiano Ronaldo, and other world-class players reportedly were exposed to the Coerver Method as young players.

This pedagogical approach made sense to Byer and was a good fit with Japanese parents. The Coerver Method, at least the first phase of it, didn't require large fields or teams of kids. Give a child a ball. Show him or her the moves. Then off they go to perfect them on their own.

Byer's camps and clinics continued to evolve, his reach expanding, and in 1993 he opened his first soccer school. Soon his schools were teaching 20,000 kids a year. In 1996, Japan was named host country of the 2002 men's World Cup, and businesses in the country moved to ramp up interest in the sport. Byer was hired to host a two-minute spot on *Oha Suta,* Japan's top-rated children's morning show, bringing his training methods to millions of kids each morning. Around the same time, he landed a deal to appear in a two-page panel in *KoroKoro Komikku,* Japan's biggest children's comic book, with a monthly circulation at the time of well over a million.

Watching him on the kids' show, standing next to a talking cartoon soccer ball, explaining in Japanese how to execute a pullback, almost always dressed in an Adidas warmup (one of his sponsors), it is clear that Byer was enjoying himself, leaning into his new persona: "Tomsan."

"Our father had that same charisma," Renée says. "My father was a really good musician, playing everything by ear, playing the accordion by ear. He could be the life of any party. Tom's got that . . . and he has had it since he was eight or nine. Even back then, everyone would say he was going to be famous someday. Not sure how famous, but famous in some way."

Byer became more than a soccer instructor; he evolved into one of Japan's best-known sports figures. In one well-worn anecdote from 2009, French star Zinedine Zidane put on a coaching clinic in Tokyo at Ajinomoto Stadium, and, as the clinic began, parents and children in the stands began chanting a name, but it wasn't Zidane's. "Tomsan, Tomsan, Tomsan," they chanted.

As Byer staged his clinics and opened his schools, as his lessons spread on TV and in comic books, Japan experienced an unmistakable improvement in the quality of the male and female players it produced. Keisuke Honda (who played for AC Milan), Tadanari Lee (Southampton), and Shinji Kagawa (Manchester United) are among the male players influenced by Tomsan. Aya Miyama, a star for Japan's women's national team, also credited Byer for her development. Kagawa in particular was the kind of gifted technical player that has long been absent from the U.S. men's pipeline.

Byer's impact did not go unnoticed. He would bring his clinics to Australia and Indonesia, and, in 2012, the Chinese Football Association named him a technical advisor and cut a deal to have him boost soccer in that country, just as he had in Japan. But even as his influence was spreading, even as he was meeting with star players in Europe and getting the approval of the head of the German Football Association and others, the soccer powers in the U.S. never gave him so much as a nod. Here was a New Yorker who helped revolutionize how countries develop their players, and yet in his homeland he was a nobody.

Then came Couva.

Tom Byer watched the U.S. lose to Trinidad and Tobago. Then he—like many fans of the sport in his native land—watched ESPN's Taylor Twellman deliver a rant in a postgame broadcast that quickly went viral. Twellman railed against the arrogance of people running the sport in the U.S. despite no real accomplishments, no World Cups won, no place at the table with the world's best.

"If this failure does not wake up everyone from U.S. Soccer to Major League Soccer, from Pay-to-Play to broadcasters, to everything, then we are all insane. Because the definition of insanity is doing the exact same thing knowing the result," Twellman said. "And if we don't change, and I mean we, everyone in U.S. Soccer, then what are we doing? What's the point? The gloves should have been off years ago. . . . What are we doing!? What are we doing!?"

At the end of his rant, Twellman was asked to provide an upside. He referenced how, after subpar showings in the 1998 World Cup and 2000 European Championship, Germany embarked on a complete rethinking of how it identified and developed soccer talent. This reimagining of how to cultivate great players—detailed painstakingly in the book *Das Reboot: How German Football Reinvented Itself and Conquered the World* by Raphael Honigstein—included a top-to-bottom reform of the German development system.

Germany—a country already vastly superior to the U.S. at developing talent, winner at that time of three World Cups and three European Championships—watched its men's national team get ousted in the quarterfinals and then the group stage in back-to-back events, and decided to rethink everything about how it developed players. Surely the U.S., after failing to make a World Cup out of a qualifying region mostly devoid of soccer powers, would do the same. That was what Twellman and so many other followers of the sport were calling for: a good hard look in the mirror. "We have an arrogance like we know what the answer is," Twellman said on ESPN the day after the loss to Trinidad. "We have to realize that our culture, that we can't do soccer the American way."

About two weeks after Couva, Tom Byer landed in Seattle. He felt, in that moment, a mix of emotions. Vindicated, of course, because finally the leaders of soccer in his homeland—including Sunil Gulati, president of U.S. Soccer at the time—had reached out and asked for his help. Maybe a little apprehensive, given the enormous task before him, helping to fix the broken U.S. system. But most of all he was giddy, because Byer is always giddy when talking about Soccer Starts at Home, because nothing juices him like spreading his gospel, and now he would finally get to do it in America.

Some within U.S. Soccer viewed the failure to qualify for

the World Cup as a blip, a confluence of unfortunate circumstances. There was no cause for alarm, they insisted. Others believed it was the dam finally breaking, and now a great reckoning was at hand. What everyone agreed was that to do nothing—or, more to the point, to *look* like you were doing nothing—would not fly.

Long before Couva, U.S. Soccer had announced it was putting $3 million toward growing the sport; it was called the Innovate to Grow Fund. The money would go to "new and innovative programs to stimulate growth." After Couva, a program with Byer was quickly added to the fund's initiatives and touted in news reports. Influential soccer writer Grant Wahl wrote in *Sports Illustrated* that "Byer's long-awaited return to America could cause a sea change in the way young soccer players develop their skills around the country." The details of the deal, as Wahl revealed later, indicated more of a toe in the water than a plunge. Byer would get $100,000 ($75,000 from U.S. Soccer and $25,000 from the Washington Youth Soccer Association) to create a Soccer Starts at Home pilot program in the U.S.

Still, it was something—a sign that the sport's leaders were heeding the call to look outward for answers, that perhaps an American reboot was coming.

In Seattle, Byer got to work spreading the gospel of Soccer Starts at Home, doing his presentation, putting together clinics, meeting with coaches and parents. In his eyes, it was a huge success. But at the end of his initial six-month agreement, U.S. Soccer offered no further funding, effectively ending the program. In his conversations with U.S. Soccer officials in charge of coaching education, Byer says they kept asking how they could quantify the results of his pilot program. How do you judge an education program aimed at kids ages two to six after only six months? "You can't," Byer says. Soccer Starts at Home is, if anything, a long game. It will take years before the kids introduced to soccer "The Byer Way" reach an age when their impact on the development pipeline is felt.

"It was a big political mess," he says.

But amid that mess was a silver lining: People in the U.S. learned more about Byer, about his work, via articles about the Soccer Starts at Home pilot program and a segment about him on *60 Minutes*. One of them was Brian Ching, the former U.S. national team striker and MLS player with the Houston Dynamo. The Dynamo had also recently hired John Walker as team president. He had a background in the NBA; he'd worked for the Memphis Grizzlies and the Phoenix Suns. Walker didn't arrive with calcified notions about how a team's youth setup should look. That trio—a popular former player inspired after reading about Byer's work, an academy director looking to remake an area's player development, and an open-minded lead executive—had no political motives. They were simply looking for ways to create better players in southeast Texas.

Byer signed a three-year contract with the Dynamo. Almost immediately, he started presenting to parents and coaches, bringing his Soccer Starts at Home methodology to Houston-area clubs.

One of the challenges Byer has always faced is that team and federation officials can't easily find a box to put him in. He's not a manager. He's not best used standing on a sideline coaching a game. He's also no longer a technical coach. In his early coaching days in Japan, that's how he would have been labeled, but as he moved his focus to the youngest kids, to Soccer Starts at Home, it no longer really applies. He made a visit to Atlanta United once, he says, and they put him with the players and coaches in that MLS team's academy, players far too old and coaches too focused on those older kids to benefit from Soccer Starts at Home. "When you get to that level they just pat you on the back and say, 'That's great.'"

His work now is "mostly about knowledge transfer," and that isn't an easy sell to those holding the checkbook, like administrators at big Pay-to-Play clubs. "I've done my presentation to hundreds and hundreds of different groups. Depending upon who's sitting in front of me, I know exactly what it is they want to see. I know exactly what slide they're going to react to. And when the business people, people who aren't on the technical side, see it they say kind of fast, 'How do you make money off this? What's the business model?'"

The Dynamo didn't ask that.

"People don't realize that professional academies are finishing schools. They bring in the best players and they basically develop them into professional players. They don't take a kid who's never touched a ball and develop him," Byer says. "Everybody thinks that Lionel Messi's development happened the first day he showed up to La Masia [in Barcelona at thirteen]. I'm talking about what Messi did when he first started to walk.

"That's the part that's really the missing link in America. They start too late. Soccer doesn't start at home."

In Houston, the goal isn't to create great players out of the

; it is to elevate the level of play of all the area's kids, to deepen the pool of talent. And you only do that by changing the way *all* children are introduced to the sport. "The only way to really make the best players better is by making the least developed players better," Byer said.

There was a potential scenario where the failure in Couva would have prompted U.S. Soccer to create a national initiative to get Soccer Starts at Home in front of all of America's families. The pilot program in Seattle would have eventually been introduced to other state associations and, funded by the federation, it would have been shared with club after club in state after state. Parent education events like the one Byer did would have been part of every club's introductory offerings to members. In addition, U.S. Soccer could have tried to reach kids where they are—in schools, using TV shows and gaming platforms, on social media—similar to what Japan did before the 2002 World Cup. It would have been expensive. It would have required time to take hold. Pay-to-Play clubs (probably) couldn't have monetized it. It also would have taken at least half a dozen years before the effectiveness of that nationwide program could be quantified, before a far greater slice of the youngest players arrived with a propensity for handling the ball rather than an instinct to send it away.

Instead, more than two years after the failure in Couva, the push to reform soccer in the U.S. at the youngest level seemed like little more than one very enthusiastic guy in a Dynamo warmup shirt standing before seventy or so parents in an elementary school outside Houston.

"This is the first domino," Byer says, never to be deterred.

"I think what's going to happen is that because we're having success here and these guys have bought in, there's going to be a model now."

It was around 6:00 P.M. when Byer left the elementary school, riding in a car driven by Holocher. As the car sped down Kingsley Drive it passed a small park off to the right, which was tucked against a small man-made lake. There were two soccer goals in the park and the faint outline of a lined field; street after street of cookie-cutter houses were nearby.

This was a neighborhood field.

Down on the grass, a man and a boy were standing about ten yards apart. The boy was no older than five or six, and the man, likely the child's father, was passing him the ball.

Here was everything Byer had just presented on, teed-up for review. A father was teaching soccer to his very young child. How would he do it? What would he emphasize? When the ball arrived, would the boy put his foot on it, maybe do some toe taps and bell touches, maybe try a pull-back or two? One mile from where Byer had given his presentation, here was a live look at America's entry level.

The father passed his son the ball, and as soon as it got near him, the boy kicked that ball as hard and as far as he could. The father then fetched the ball and they did it again. Over and over and over.

Talking about that scene later, Byer displays not even a hint of discouragement. "Oh, we'll reach that parent," he says. "We will."

6

SHIFTING THE PARADIGM
A generation finally gets the right kind of coaching

The video is, by now, part of American soccer lore. At 12 minutes and 29 seconds long, the clip is from a game in the 2012 Cal South State Cup, when Barcelona USA's U-11 team faced a team from Arsenal FC, a successful Southern California club. The Barcelona USA players are pinging the ball around as if they are the real Barcelona. They are not just dominating Arsenal FC, a side with considerable talent, but doing it with skill and precision and a remarkable understanding of space.

When the video surfaced, it created a stir. Few American teams with boys so young played that way. Many aspired to, of course, but few pulled it off. And the video was only a snapshot of what that Barcelona USA team did to almost every domestic opponent. The group also went overseas and competed in prestigious tournaments, hanging with and

sometimes defeating academy teams from Barcelona, Atlé-
tico Madrid, Manchester United, and other giant clubs.
Coaches from those European teams were astonished that a
team of young American boys could play the game just as
their young players did. On the field were a young Efraín
Álvarez, a young Uly Llanez, a young Alex Mendez. Álvarez
would eventually sign with the L.A. Galaxy, Llanez with
Wolfsburg in the Bundesliga, Mendez with SC Freiburg in
Germany. Several others on the team would go on to play in
college.

Explaining how that occurred—how Barcelona USA's
group of young kids learned to play that way, and what a rare
occurrence it was—requires some context.

When AYSO's founders met in 1964 in Torrance, they
talked about nearly every aspect of the game. They regulated
playing-time minimums and roster size. They put rules in
place governing where practices and games could be staged,
so that children and parents didn't need to travel far to participate. They mandated that team names make no reference
to ethnicity, and they made sure that the organization's first
president was a "real" American. Later, they also implemented
a fee structure that would make the game affordable.

Notice what they didn't spend much time on?

Coaching.

For all the thought given to how to spread the game across
the United States, AYSO's founders gave little consideration
to how the game would be taught to kids. The first leaders of
the organization were well-versed in soccer; they likely had
an idea of how *they* would teach the game. But for the parents being handed teams, there was little to no guidance.

This may have been intentional: AYSO's leaders needed parental involvement—dads and moms on the sidelines—and recruiting them would have been more difficult if AYSO had implemented coaching standards or required a coaching license. Any parent with enthusiasm and a willingness to take on the commitment could become a soccer coach; actual knowledge of the game or how to teach it was secondary.

So, in the late 1960s, when a dad with no soccer background was handed a team in his local league, what did he do?

"He reaches for what worked in other sports, what worked in baseball or football or basketball," says Todd Beane, founder of the TOVO Institute/Academy, a coach and player training center in Barcelona. "I am old enough to have seen several movements within the game in the U.S., and the first was coaches believing that what worked in other sports could work for soccer."

Beane grew up in the Northeast, playing ice hockey and baseball as a young boy living outside Boston. He moved to New Hampshire for middle school, and that was the first time he played soccer. Born in 1964, he was among the early generation of players cultured under "The American Way."

The coaching he received at first was "a pure fitness approach," he says, which was not unusual. The go-to for coaches who didn't know the game was to run the crap out of kids. In the late 1960s and '70s, youth soccer players spent far less time touching the ball than they did hauling across grass fields, their lungs and legs burning, a dad urging them to go harder and farther. What little ball work was taught was conveyed via drills that were modified activities from another sport. "Circuit-type drills and line drills were dominant," Beane says. "Okay, we'll do passing now. We will do dribbling now. We will do shooting now. And mostly that meant line up, execute a shot, and go back to the end of the line. Line up, pass the ball, now go to the end of the line. Line up, and here comes a ball, head the ball if you can, and then go back in the line."

Beane's coach at Simsbury High School in Connecticut from 1978 to 1981 was Jack Wilson, "a baseball coach who, out of the goodness of his heart, took on coaching this group of kids," Beane says. Unsurprisingly, Wilson tried to teach soccer the baseball way. "His thinking was, *Hey, I've got to isolate the skill and teach it.* That works for ground balls, fly balls, double plays, and everything else in baseball. So we did line drills that were taken from baseball. Maybe we scrimmaged a little at the end of practice, and that was the closest we got to an actual soccer activity."

This was happening across the country in the 1970s and into the 1980s as (mostly) men with backgrounds in other sports took over youth and high school soccer teams. Kids were not really learning to play but rather learning isolated skills that, the coaches hoped, would lead to some sort of collective performance. And no one knew enough to say that what they were doing was wrong. Jack Wilson won a state soccer title for Simsbury High in 1981, Beane's senior season. Who was going to say back then that what Wilson was doing was incorrect?

In 1982, Beane enrolled at Dartmouth College, and there he experienced the second movement in coaching in the U.S. His coach for the first three years was Tom Griffith—Coach Griff—who took the approach of a typical American coach. Then, before Beane's senior year, the school hired Bobby Clark, a former goalkeeper from Scotland who had played professionally in the Scottish League. In hiring Clark, Dartmouth was following a trend, as colleges and youth clubs had begun looking to the United Kingdom for coaches.

"The English and Scottish influence quickly permeated at least all of the upper portion of soccer in the United States from coast to coast," Beane says. "Now, whether or not all of the coaches that came over were qualified in any shape or form is probably to be debated. Some were, some were not. But in any case, they only brought one brand of football with them, this British bang-and-bruise type of game, which was English football at the time."

To play that way, these coaches looked for a certain type of player. "A boy with character, a boy with athleticism, and a boy willing to get stuck in," Beane says. "And that's what they found. And that's what they nurtured. Unfortunately, that came at the detriment to other boys who were less physical, potentially more skillful, and also had great character but were not the big, strong, strapping lad."

Clark was a successful college coach; he later led teams at Stanford and Notre Dame, which won a national championship in 2013 under Clark's leadership. So, again, who was to say that the type of player he favored, and the way he (and many others) coached, was wrong?

The emphasis on fitness in the 1960s and '70s, blended with the influence of coaches from the United Kingdom in the 1980s, created what would become the quintessential American player: athletic, powerful, willing to run and grind and commit to the physical nature of the game. And, tactically, the way soccer was played in England and Scotland in the 1980s became the dominant style in the U.S. "It bled through the NCAA ranks and then down into the youth game," Beane says. "And remember that in the 1980s the college system was the upper echelon of soccer in the U.S. That was where my generation of players aspired to play. Very few players were bypassing college for opportunities in Europe or elsewhere, so everyone was going to college and learning one way to play."

When it came to the USMNT, the majority of the players selected were products of the college system, so that homogeneousness carried over. "It is possible that in some regions there was some Latin influence, maybe a little bit more skillful approach to the game," Beane says. "But without a doubt, and even still to this day, the English and Scottish influence was incredibly powerful, and it influenced every aspect of how we approached the game, and how we trained the game."

After college, Beane played three seasons of semi-pro soccer with the Reno Rattlers of the United Systems of Independent Soccer Leagues, then coached at a youth club in New Hampshire. As a coach in the 1990s, Beane became part of a third coaching movement. Around that time, coaches in the U.S. woke up to the fact that their players were far less skilled than foreign opponents, even those from much smaller countries.

Perhaps it was seeing the U.S. struggle in the 1990 World Cup, its first appearance in that event in forty years. The U.S. lost to Czechoslovakia, Austria, and host Italy by a combined score of 8–2. Or maybe it was in 1994, when the U.S. hosted the World Cup and fared better, but American coaches got to see creative players like Romário, Carlos Valderrama, Gheorghe Hagi, and others up close. Their skill with the ball was unmistakably un-American. The changing nature of the game in England may have also been an influence, as former Arsenal coach Arsène Wenger and others pushed the Premier League further from the style the U.S. had imported. Some or all of those factors prompted a collective realization among coaches that they had to expand what they were doing.

Remember the Coerver Method, the developmental philosophy that Tom Byer subscribed to, the one that taught specific moves to young players? In the 1990s, U.S. coaches attending clinics and conferences began to discuss that approach, even if they didn't call it by that name.

"I think it was an honest recognition and a simple recognition that we were not as skillful as the world's best. So the priority was to fill that gap through technical skill training," Beane says. "Everybody on the ball, everybody working their moves, and everybody executing their moves so that we could catch up to the world in technical ability. It was a clear agenda. It was a well-intended agenda. And it just swept across the country."

This emphasis was not, as it might seem, a threat to the English and Scottish influence on America's development system. Nor did it have to come at the expense of the aerobic emphasis that had been around since the late 1960s. "The thinking was that it would complement it all," Beane says. "Fitness plus athleticism plus skill, it sounds like an amazing formula for success. And so we all embraced that whole-

rtedly, and thought it would fill the gap that was prevalent
at the international stage between us and other countries."

It didn't fill the gap, of course, with the vast majority of
U.S. players who emerged in the 1990s and the early 2000s
still predominantly strapping lads who were fit and aggressive and athletic but, despite more time on the ball in training, still lacked creativity and played a version of the game
stuck in time. "Even with the emphasis on 'hey, every child
needs a ball,' the focus was still athleticism first, fitness second, and ball mastery third," Beane says.

In 2002, Beane moved to Spain and helped found the
Cruyff Institute for Sport Studies, which, among other services, helped professional clubs revamp their academies, in
terms of both soccer instruction and academic offerings. It
was headed by Johan Cruyff, the famous Dutch player who had
also managed Ajax (1985–1988) and Barcelona (1988–1996).

Cruyff popularized the concept of Total Football. This
tactical approach—first tried in the 1930s in Austria—was
attack-minded but possession-oriented. Players were positioned in the usual spots (defenders, midfielders, forwards),
but whether they stayed in those spots depended on the situation. Positions were fluid. A defender might push forward
into attack, and then a midfielder fill the space he'd vacated.
Total Football players had to be multifaceted. A forward
couldn't just be good at, say, winning aerial duels or hold-up
play. A defender couldn't only be adept at tackling or man-
marking. Everyone on the field had to possess exceptional
soccer ability and instincts.

While at Barcelona, Cruyff also founded the club's youth
academy, La Masia, and he introduced the idea that every

player in the academy, regardless of age, should be trained the same way. He aimed to create a consistent philosophy and style of play, so that the players who ascended to the first team would be better prepared when they got there. Much of the success Barcelona experienced in the 2000s, and Spain's winning of the World Cup in 2010, has been attributed to the philosophies ingrained by Cruyff.

Cruyff and Beane became close; in 2008, Beane married Cruyff's daughter, Chantal. He and Cruyff spent countless hours talking about the game, the way it was instructed in Europe and in the U.S., and it led Beane to reflect on his own experience. Among his conclusions:

"My generation and generations after me never got a real understanding of the game."

Brian Kleiban was part of one of those lost generations.

He was born in 1979, fifteen years after Todd Beane, and was raised across the country in La Mirada, a then middle-class suburb in southeast Los Angeles County. Yet the coaching he got as a young player mostly mirrors what Beane received.

Kleiban played in his local AYSO league. "We were coached by players' parents, and they did the best they could," Kleiban says. When he was around thirteen, after years dominating that league, Kleiban's parents moved him to a club in Mission Viejo, but the trek was too far and it was too expensive. He then played at St. Paul High in Santa Fe Springs. "My coaches there were a math teacher or a science teacher who were just doing it for the stipend and to help out. They were great people, but they didn't have a clue about coaching."

In 1998, Kleiban walked on at Cal State Fullerton, but left
the team after a month and headed to Argentina, where his
parents had emigrated from, "to see if I was as good as I
thought I was." He finagled a tryout with Central Córdoba,
in the third tier of soccer in Argentina. "That's where it hit
me that I wasn't going to make a living playing soccer."

Back in Southern California in 1999, twenty years old
and not sure what he would do with his life, he connected
with a friend who was coaching a team of teenagers at a
small club in Orange County. He eventually took over despite little coaching experience, among the generations of
players-turned-coaches who lacked a real understanding of
the game. But Kleiban was also young, and his Argentinian
heritage made him more aware than most of how the game
could be played.

So Kleiban did what too few U.S. coaches have the time or
inclination to do: He studied the game. He analyzed various
coaching methodologies, reading books and watching the
training sessions of more experienced coaches. In 2004, he
went to Peru for a month to follow the Argentinian national
team, which at the time was managed by Marcelo Bielsa, one
of the game's most innovative coaches. "That was my role
model, that's who I looked up to," Kleiban says. Before Bielsa
took over, "Argentina was always talented, always had match
winners, but they wouldn't dominate irrelevant of the opponent, irrelevant of the venue." But under Bielsa and his famous pressing style, that changed, "and that's how I wanted
my team to look and play." During that month in Peru, Kleiban
snuck into Argentina's training sessions, pen and paper in
hand, and he took notes. Years later, when Real Madrid trained

at UCLA during a tour of the U.S., Kleiban wangled his way into those sessions as well, to observe José Mourinho.

In 2007, Kleiban was coaching at that same small club in Orange County, and yet his U-16 group won a U.S. Club national championship. *Who is this guy and what is he doing?* was being asked by more than a few club directors in Southern California. One of them was Paul Walker, who was operating Barcelona USA, an Orange County club affiliated with the Spanish professional club. Walker recruited Kleiban to Barcelona USA to coach a team of older boys.

Because of Barcelona USA's affiliation with the real Barcelona, Kleiban was permitted to travel to Spain when the clubs' teams played squads from La Masia. "And then I would stay an additional two weeks, like an internship there, to watch the whole academy makeup, from the U-9s all the way to the first team," he says. "So I'm there, I'm studying, and then everything needs to be adapted to our football here. But it pretty much was a copy of that [Total Football] philosophy, mixed in with a little bit of the high-pressing Bielsa style of football."

After Kleiban's older team aged out of youth soccer, Walker approached Kleiban with the idea for him to coach one of the club's youngest groups.

Kleiban told Walker he was crazy. He wanted to be a professional coach, and he didn't see a way to get there by coaching the youngest kids. "All I am thinking is I don't want to be out there teaching young kids the proper way to kick a ball," Kleiban says.

Walker asked him to watch Barcelona USA's team of eight- and nine-year-olds train before nixing the idea.

"It was on a field in South Central Los Angeles, a really bad area, and these kids started showing up with their balls, passing to each other," Kleiban says. About 90 percent of the team was Latino, a departure from the team of predominantly white kids Kleiban had been coaching. "And they were just outrageously talented. I was blown away." He saw an opportunity to teach Total Football "to these kids who were a blank canvas."

If a less knowledgeable coach had attended one of Kleiban's training sessions, they might have been surprised by the simplicity of his approach. Practices started with a 4v1 rondo (a version of keep-away), two touches mandatory. Then a 4v1 rondo with one touch to work on their technique. Next came a simple positional possession game, for relationship building, with players going toward a mini-goal or an end line to get points. And then came small-sided games (3v3, 4v4, 5v5), so the players got as many touches as possible.

Within that simply designed practice was "massive intensity," Kleiban says. And everything was laid out so there was a smooth transition from one exercise to the next. There were no long water breaks where kids engaged with their parents. During those ninety-minute sessions, "it was all business."

"A lot of coaches, especially at the younger ages, want to do ten thousand different drills. They don't want to repeat themselves, thinking it will keep the kids engaged," Kleiban says. "We were quite the opposite. It was about simple repetitions of the basic fundamentals. So everything starts with the rondo, receiving the ball the right way, honing your technique, not limiting yourself by receiving with the wrong foot. And when you start teaching these things to these guys at eight or nine, young players who are already technically very sound, they love it. And it's all about creating an environment where they take pride in taking care of the ball."

So what happens when the long-standing American coaching methodologies are thrown out the window, when a "blank canvas" of kids are presented with the knowledge Kleiban has accumulated?

"What happened is what people saw in the video," Kleiban says, referring to that U-11 team that impressed so many.

When the boys reached U-13, they were eligible to play in the Development Academy, the league of elite clubs started by the U.S. Soccer Federation in 2007. Barcelona USA was not in the Development Academy, so Kleiban took most of the roster to the academy of Chivas USA, an MLS club based in Los Angeles. When Chivas USA folded in 2014, he moved the group to the L.A. Galaxy academy.

Reflecting on Kleiban's work with that group of kids, one could view what he did as extremely hopeful: *Look what is possible when young players in the U.S. are chosen based not on their pure athleticism or size or where they live, but rather on their ability; and when they get good coaching; and when they are taught the game and not just individual skills.* But there is something bittersweet about it, too, because of the decades of players, loaded with talent and desire, who never got that chance.

"We have quality here in America, and we always have had quality," Kleiban says. "We just would turn a blind eye, or we didn't have people working with them at a young age to give them the basic fundamentals, and kind of teach them t the level is around the world. When that does happen, you can produce something unique and special."

Todd Beane is hopeful.

Not just because U.S. coaches are becoming more and more like Brian Kleiban, though he believes that is happening. Since he founded TOVO in 2015, Beane has lectured and taught in the U.S., and also welcomed coaches and players from America to the TOVO facility in Spain. He believes another coaching movement is underway in the U.S. "For many years, and even across fields throughout the United States today, the technical-centric paradigm has been omnipresent." That needs to shift to a "cognitive technical paradigm," he says, and many American coaches are beginning to make that transition. "And what I mean by cognitive technical paradigm is to really consider soccer as a game of finding and exploiting space. And to see that our responsibility as a coach is to facilitate our players' ability to find and exploit space. Finding space is about vision, and exploiting space is about precision. And that's where that technical-centric paradigm fails, because it's only about precision. A cognitive technical paradigm is about vision and precision."

What does that paradigm shift look like in practical terms, in the construct of a typical practice? Drills, if they are done, should be done in context. Don't have a player do a move against a cone or a dummy; have them do it against another player. Small-sided games are vital. They can accelerate the vision and understanding of space that players need, while also giving them more opportunities to exploit that space because they get more time with and around the ball.

Something as simple as a rondo, the drill Brian Kleiban started each practice with (and which Johan Cruyff brought to Barcelona), helps players learn how to find and exploit space.

Some of that has permeated coaching culture in the U.S., but that is not the only reason Beane believes future generations of American players will be better off.

"When I go around the United States now, the kids know more about soccer and the players playing the game, where they're playing, how they play the game, who's coaching the game. The kids are more knowledgeable because they are connected digitally, and armed with this information, they're taking charge. They're not waiting for Mom and Dad. They're not waiting for a club coach who may be two decades behind. They're downloading their future aspirations and building their own microcultures without us. They have clarity about what they want, and they're going to get it whether we provide it for them or not."

After decades of U.S. coaches generally failing to teach kids the proper way to play the game, the kids are no longer settling for that.

"That is reason to have great optimism, because they are going to create their own paths," Beane says. "And the ones that are now just getting into club football, and just in their early teens, are going to be even better than the generation we're seeing now, the [Christian] Pulisics and the [Weston] McKennies, because these young players are not stopping and they're not waiting for anybody."

III

In early 2011, Matt Carver was doing what any good lawyer does: He was looking for a precedent.

At the time, he was locked in a paper war with the Iowa Soccer Association (ISA). After forming the J-Hawk Soccer Club in 2010, Carver applied to have J-Hawk become affiliated with ISA, a seemingly routine application process that would allow J-Hawk to play in local leagues. His application was denied.

"Basically, the response was: There was no need for you. There's already another club there," Carver said. "I wasn't anticipating that. I believed that we would immediately get affiliated."

Carver wondered if he wasn't just being made to work a little harder for affiliation—his penance for challenging the Urbandale Soccer Club, which had long-standing ties with the ISA. "I thought, well, we would all get together and work it out as adults." Carver filed a request to reconsider, but in October 2010 his application was again denied.

The reasoning behind that denial, written by ISA's executive director Harold Kahler, included five points supporting ISA's position, but the five are different versions of the same answer: J-Hawk's presence was detrimental to the existing clubs.

Carver started J-Hawk with two girls' teams—a U-12 group (daughter Maddie's team) and a U-14 squad (Jessi's team)—

but because ISA refused to allow J-Hawk to affiliate, those teams could not play in local leagues. They played friendlies and entered tournaments when the hosting club would allow it, but Carver's group of kids had been effectively banned from playing organized soccer in Iowa. The kids and parents often had to drive as far as Kansas City and Omaha to find games.

That was why in 2011 he was digging deep on the United States Soccer Federation's website, looking through its list of rulings on various grievances involving youth clubs around the country, reading decision after decision. He wanted to know that if he started a fight with ISA, he could win it.

In 2001, a youth soccer club in Washington State—Columbia Basin Soccer Academy (CBSA)—hoped to form some competitive teams. Its application with the local association was rejected because, as the association later stated, there was already a competitive club in the region, and CBSA would have a "detrimental impact" on the existing competitive club. When CBSA fought the local organization's decision, the matter made its way through the federation's grievance process, ending with a hearing before an arbitrator appointed by USSF's board of directors.

The arbitrator ruled against Columbia Basin Soccer Academy, but it would be inaccurate to say the club lost. CBSA had asked to join the local league *before* its competitive teams were formed. The arbitrator ruled that the CBSA had nothing to grieve until it had actually put together a team and was denied. But within that decision, USSF made it clear that if CBSA actually formed competitive teams, it had to be allowed "a mechanism for affiliation." And, most significantly, the board rejected the notion that a club "can be turned away because [a state association] determines that there is no 'need' for the club in a certain area."

When Matt Carver read that decision on the U.S. Soccer website, his eyes lit up. He had found a precedent.

Carver sent the Columbia Basin decision to Kahler and others at the Iowa Soccer Association; he let it be known that the USSF had already invalidated the reasoning ISA was using to deny J-Hawk affiliation. He hoped the "adults" could sort it out. But ISA held firm.

Even without a league to put his teams in, Carver continued to build J-Hawk, and in fall 2011 he created teams at the youngest divisions, U-5 through U-8. He charged only $25 to $40 a season (depending on the age group), or about half of what USC charged, and he streamlined the process for families to get scholarships. At many clubs, that process requires filling out time-consuming financial disclosure forms. Not all clubs offer them in a language other than English, and sometimes they can only be found online. And, of course, it is not lost on parents that they are disclosing their financial struggles to people in the community—like board members—and that can stigmatize kids, those "scholarship" players. In Carver's eyes, those forms and that process were a barrier to kids playing soccer. So he cut right through it. If a parent registering their child at the J-Hawk Soccer Club couldn't pay the registration fee, they merely had to write "scholarship" anywhere on their registration form, and it was done.

In its first eighteen months in existence, the J-Hawk Soccer Club registered more than two hundred kids. Carver did considerable outreach to schools, connecting with ESL teachers to make it known that the club was open to children from all backgrounds. "I thought when we started we would get more kids from families who, maybe for cultural reasons, hadn't felt comfortable enrolling with USC," Carver says. But the first wave consisted mostly of white kids from working families who had either been priced out of soccer or did not feel welcome at other clubs.

As J-Hawk entered its second year of existence, Carver pushed to resolve the lack of affiliation, appealing directly to U.S. Soccer. He wrote email after email—including several to Sunil Gulati, then the president of the USSF. "U.S. Soccer knew the precedent and I sent them ISA's responses. They knew it was wrong, and I was just saying, 'Why don't you just police this?'" Carver was informed that he would have to file a formal grievance. *Okay, I'm a lawyer, I can do this,* he thought. But then he was told that when the matter reached arbitration he would be responsible for a third of the cost, approximately $3,700.

He wrote to U.S. Soccer: "We have a clear violation here. We're raising money to try to buy soccer goals at this point, and you're going to make us pay $3,700?" Carver didn't have the money, so he again appealed to ISA via email. Perhaps enough penance had been paid.

He would do that often—reach out and ask if ISA had changed its mind. He'd update ISA on his registration numbers. He'd send team photos. Nothing he did mattered. J-Hawk remained unaffiliated. And, in a stunning bit of irony, the repeated rejection emails Carver got from ISA included, at the bottom, ISA's motto:

Let the Kids Play!

Carver kept growing the club, working as best he could around the lack of affiliation. By fall 2014, J-Hawk consisted of more than three hundred kids. The children from underserved communities that he thought would initially flock to the club eventually found it. One year, J-Hawk's U-11 team featured nine first-generation kids. Later, that same team would include thirteen children from families that had recently immigrated to the United States. "And this is happening in a suburb of Des Moines," Carver says. "Think about that."

One of Carver's players, Recardo Wleh, was from Liberia. Carver's son Max had met Wleh at school and recruited him. Wleh had been separated from his parents, staying in Liberia for years while they carved out a life in the United States. Once he joined his parents in Iowa, he struggled with the transition. "He had played soccer in Liberia, and he was the best player, but emotionally he was going through some things," Carver says. Carver built a relationship with Wleh and his family, and Wleh connected with teammates whose parents had immigrated to the United States from Iraq, Bosnia, Laos, Mexico, and elsewhere. Later, Wleh would play for Sporting Kansas City's academy team, and Carver paid the $400 fee so Wleh could live with a host family in Kansas City.

Another J-Hawk kid was Carver's youngest son, Rockne. In the basement of their house, little Rockne would dribble a mini-ball around, soccer starting at home. As Carver began coaching Rockne and his young teammates, he instructed them differently. He had learned so much about coaching since working with his older kids' teams. Now it was rondos and short-sided games, all efforts made to teach them to find space and exploit it.

Around Urbandale, Carver was "an insider suddenly treated like an outsider." He'd walk into a room and feel the conversation suddenly change. "There was just this look I'd get." *Hate* is a word Carver doesn't like to just throw around, but "it was fairly intense dislike." People were dismayed that he was upsetting the order of things and bringing different players into the local soccer ecosystem, kids who were often better than their own kids. After seeing the movie *The Purge*— a dystopian horror film that imagines a twelve-hour period where all crimes, including murder, are allowed—one of Carver's kids joked, "Dad, if that happens here you are in trouble."

Multiple times, Carver showed up at Martin Field (J-Hawk's only soccer field) and found the nets cut. He had to get permission from the neighboring police precinct to store his smaller goals in their parking lot. Once, he found his car in his driveway with a flat tire. When he got the tire replaced, the mechanic found a screw and a razor blade in the rubber. Five days later, he found another screw in his tire. His mother's car, parked in front of his house, also got a screw in one of its tires. "To whomever vandalized my car, let me be clear, we will not be deterred," he wrote on Facebook. He couldn't help but think back to his time in Germany and how the village took great pride in the cultivation of young players. In Urbandale, that pride seemed to surround only a certain type of player from a certain type of family. Everyone else was, as Mike Carver had predicted, a threat.

By 2015, J-Hawk registered close to four hundred kids, from U-5 to U-14. After J-Hawk reduced fees for recreational play, the Urbandale Soccer Club lowered its own recreational fees, and its registration numbers rose. J-Hawk's presence had increased competition for players, which resulted in a lowering of the cost of participating across the area, which in turn brought in more kids overall. And yet, ISA continued to deny J-Hawk affiliation.

To maintain that stance, ISA had to brush aside an immense amount of evidence of Matt Carver's success: Carver, a native son of Urbandale and the child of a former councilman, started a soccer club for the stated purpose of making the sport more accessible to more kids. He was a qualified coach—he had his state D-license—and he had played three years on a semi-pro team in Germany. He was also a member of the Iowa State Bar Association and a veteran who still served in the National Guard. Every Sunday, you'd find him in a pew at Westchester Evangelical Free Church.

J-Hawk itself had become an entry point for children from poor families, and the children of immigrants, and it helped retain kids who likely would have left the sport if they hadn't been offered an alternative to Pay-to-Play. By operating J-Hawk as a true nonprofit, charging kids only what it cost to operate their teams, Carver had also brought down the cost of soccer at Urbandale's other club.

Seeing all of that, the stance of the Iowa Soccer Association remained, incredibly, that J-Hawk was bad for soccer in Iowa.

CASA GRANDE

MLS finds its place in the development pyramid

When he was around eleven or twelve years old, Trevor Hyman began taking soccer more seriously. It was 2007, and he was doing well for his local club, the Irvine Strikers, but he felt he should be looking for more. He moved to another Orange County club, West Coast FC, which had one of the best teams in the country in his age group. It just seemed like that was where a player with ambition should be. While playing for that club, he won two state cups and won regionals twice, and he was evolving into a very nice player, a box-to-box center midfielder with good passing range and limitless stamina. The coaches at the University of California at Irvine were aware of him; he attended their camps and they recognized his talent. He also showed well in the U.S. Youth Soccer Olympic Development Program (ODP)—tryouts and camps run by state associations that, since 1977, had been the primary tool for identifying elite talent in America.

Hyman was on what has long been the traditional pathway for a top player in the United States: a well-off kid from the suburbs emerging from a Pay-to-Play club, being evaluated and scouted in ODP, and then moving on from there, likely to a college program. This is unlike the pathway in most developed soccer nations, particularly those in Europe. There, young players are typically identified by a professional club early, often at ten years old or younger. Even though players cannot sign professional contracts until they are teenagers (seventeen in the United Kingdom, for example), kids are trained by coaches affiliated with the pro team. This might happen at the professional club in a player's hometown, in which case the player would live at home. But young players regularly move to bigger clubs farther away, because they are constantly being scouted, and in those cases they typically live with a host family or in a residency academy paid for and operated by the pro team. In European academies, every aspect of a player's life (including their academic work) is structured to accommodate training and competitive play. Though the youngest kids may not technically be "professional" players, their daily life is 100 percent directed toward that end.

Around the time Trevor Hyman reached high school, the long-standing youth development structure in America suddenly shifted. In 2007, the U.S. Soccer Federation announced the formation of the Development Academy (DA). It was an attempt to bring more structure to elite youth soccer by putting the best teams around the country (initially from U-15 up to U-17) on the same calendar and controlling who and how often they played. To be clear, the DA did not represent a takeover of elite youth soccer by the federation; it was a partnership between U.S. Soccer and influential Pay-to-Play clubs. Still, it was a seismic move by an organization that had long clung to the status quo.

That creation of the DA dovetailed with another major shift, this one in Major League Soccer. For most of its history, MLS had outsourced player development. Teams drafted college players and supplemented them with foreign talent, some expensive (like David Beckham), many of them less so. But around 2008, the league woke up to the fact that every other substantial pro league in the world developed talent, so MLS created its Homegrown Player program. This incentivized the cultivation of local players, because those signed out of a team's academy didn't count against the salary cap. This meant teams could sign young players and, even if they weren't ready to contribute right away, they wouldn't hurt the on-field product by taking up salary space. Teams also got a larger slice of the transfer fee for the sale of a Homegrown Player versus another player. It became even more profitable to develop players and sell them off to, say, a richer club in England or Italy or Germany. At times it could be fuzzy whether a player was *really* a product of a team's academy— there were geographic boundaries teams had to (somewhat) abide by, some franchises had satellite areas assigned, and some players spent very little time at an academy before signing a Homegrown contract. But the impact was that developing local talent became a priority for many MLS clubs.

Trevor's father, Scott, was tracking the development of

the DA—which MLS academy teams played in—and the league's increased focus on youth development. "I wasn't really thinking a whole lot about what my pathway was going to be," Trevor says. "I thought I was a top player in Southern California and wanted just to keep playing with whoever the best teams were, and whatnot." But his dad was focused on what the best players were doing to get to college and beyond.

Scott moved Trevor to a different Orange County club, the Pateadores Soccer Club, which played in the DA. Even as Trevor spent the 2010–2011 season there, his father was evaluating what felt like a constantly shifting landscape.

Both Scott and his wife, Gloria, are successful lawyers in Orange County, bringing to mind what David Keyes had seen north of San Diego: lines of expensive SUVs dropping kids off, young players with the latest $200 cleats, American soccer's inherent elitism. But Gloria was a first-generation Korean American whose father had been a doctor in a MASH unit during the Korean War; Scott grew up in a single-parent household in the South. Their goal for Trevor was never that he'd one day play for Manchester United or Real Madrid or even the L.A. Galaxy. It was to find out whether his soccer ability, combined with strong academic work, could help him get into a great college.

In 2010, when Trevor was a high school sophomore at Northwood High School in Irvine—the same school that produced Benny Feilhaber, a sub in the 2017 game in Couva—Scott Hyman recognized that there was a hierarchy within the Development Academy. A colleague's son was playing for the L.A. Galaxy's academy team, and "just because he was playing for the Galaxy he's getting lots of looks from colleges," Trevor says. "I mean, playing for an MLS academy team, a lot of people are going to see you."

They explored the possibility of Trevor joining the Galaxy academy, "but I was just thinking about taking four AP classes and doing a drive four or five days a week to Carson," where the Galaxy trained. That commute would require thirty miles each way on the parking lot that is the 405 Freeway. "Both my parents had jobs, and having a younger sister with her own activities, the math really did not add up in terms of trying to pull that off."

But if the goal was for Trevor to become the best player he could be, to potentially join one of the better college programs, the feeling was that they should do something. "And that was when my dad said, 'Hey, I've heard about this thing in Arizona.'"

The "thing" in Arizona is not easily described; it is best to start with what it was before detailing what it became.

In 1961, the San Francisco Giants of Major League Baseball built a spring training complex on about fifty acres in Casa Grande, a way-stop between Phoenix and Tucson on Interstate 10. It was a state-of-the-art facility devoted to the baseball experience. The swimming pool was shaped like a baseball bat, and the overhang on the hotel tower was crafted to look like the brim of a cap. After the Giants left in 1979 for a more convenient location, the California Angels moved in until 1982, when they too left for a less remote spring training base. The baseball fields were converted to football fields and a USFL team practiced there, but then that league folded and, by the late 1980s, the facility had become just another golf resort in a state full of them—but with the added challenges of being in a middle-of-nowhere town of about 50,000 people, with a somewhat dated hotel on the premises.

In 1985, a pair of successful real estate developers, Michael Saunders (a woman) and Ron Burks, bought the challenged asset. They hoped to find a use for it that would not ride "the typical booms and busts of the hotel, resort, and golf business," says Tim Alai, the general manager of the company Saunders and Burks built. Around 2007, Burks had a brainstorm: Could they develop a sports academy on the site, a West Coast version of the IMG Academy in Florida? Turn the older hotel into a dorm, build out the offices and training space, hire top coaches and staff, and then charge families hefty tuition to send their hopeful sport prodigies there? "Originally, part of the desire was to have a multi-sport, multi-gender complex, like IMG. Because of the land, the sports, the climate, there's a lot of similarities there," Alai says.

But in talking with Casa Grande city officials, it was clear that if they were to partner with the city on redeveloping the site, they would need to create grass fields, which were desperately needed for local soccer teams. Managing golf courses meant they already knew grass, so they developed six pristine grass fields with lights. But even after they were completed, soccer remained an afterthought in the grand plan, behind tennis and other sports they thought would drive revenue at their new Grande Sports World.

Then MLS started the Development Academy, and Burks and Alai realized soccer could be more central to their vision. After all, they had those beautiful lighted fields, four locker rooms, two therapy areas, and sixteen flexible class-rooms. In early 2010 they hired Greg Vanney, the former USMNT player, to build a soccer academy. "Everyone knows Greg and respects him," Alai says, and Vanney helped the facility get through the DA approval process. "And here we are in a little, little city. Yes, we had a great complex, but we didn't have players. We didn't really have any coaches at the time. We were creating it from scratch." Vanney recruited former MLS player Mike Muñoz to help him coach, and also brought in Freddy Juarez, who'd had success coaching youth teams in Las Cruces, New Mexico. By fall 2010, with their DA application approved by U.S. Soccer, the Casa Grande Academy opened and had its first team, a U-16 squad featuring several players Juarez brought from New Mexico.

Despite having only thirty kids in the entire program at that point, some living on-site and some commuting from nearby cities, word began to travel. "MLS teams were coming in for preseason training, and you had Greg and Mike and Freddy there, and it was like, what is going on there?" says John Galas, who in 2010 was the women's coach at the University of Arizona. Galas traveled up Interstate 10 to visit. "There was some talent there for sure," he continues. He began moonlighting as a coach in Casa Grande and then in 2011 was hired full-time, not long after Vanney left to coach with Chivas USA in MLS.

Casa Grande is about seven hundred miles from Salt Lake City, but that did not stop Real Salt Lake (RSL) general manager Garth Lagerwey and team president Bill Manning from seeing the potential in Grande Sports World. Utah was hardly a hotbed of soccer talent, but Arizona was, and MLS had deemed that state to be RSL territory when it drew its Home-grown lines. RSL formalized a partnership with Burks and Saunders, and with the stroke of a pen created something that had never existed in the United States: a residency academy affiliated with a professional team. They had long been the norm in more developed soccer nations, but in America what was started at Casa Grande in 2010–2011 was ground-breaking.

"There were so many eyes on what we were doing," Galas says. "U.S. Soccer officials were out there all the time." People from the Mexican Soccer Federation came by, and Martín Vásquez, who was on staff with the USMNT, joined after Muñoz left to go to Chivas with Vanney. "That was huge, that connection to the national team, and it just felt like the whole thing was us putting that flagpole in the ground and saying, 'Hey, we're serious about this program and about player development.'"

In 2011, Scott Hyman, Trevor's father, read about what was happening in Casa Grande and contacted the staff there, emailing Trevor's soccer résumé and some footage of him playing. In early summer, Trevor traveled to Arizona for a tryout. He was about to turn sixteen and entering his junior year of high school. "I had played with the ODP regional team for two years. I was one of the captains at an inter-regional event. So I felt like it was reasonable for me to say that I was definitely not just a top Southern California player, but also someone who could compete at a national level," Trevor says. At Casa Grande, "I get out there and play with the guys and, I mean, they were just so sick. Everyone was *so* good. The instruction, even for me just being there for a try-out, was so good."

While he was visiting with his mother, monsoon winds ripped off part of the roof of the hotel where the players stayed. "There was debris everywhere and my mom is thinking, 'I'm not sure this is a safe place to leave my fifteen-year-old,' but I was like, 'If they want me, I am definitely coming.'"

They were up by 6:00 A.M. for an empty-stomach run around the area surrounding the complex. Then, after an ice bath and breakfast, some players would nap and others would play small-sided games or soccer tennis. The same after lunch, plus strength training. After dinner, from about 8:30 to 10:30 P.M., they trained as a team outside under the lights, the late start required to beat the Arizona heat. "In the summer there wasn't much of anything to do but play, and we pretty much did that all day," Trevor says.

When school started in September, there was strength training in the morning before classes at a local high school. Then homework, then bolt to the performance center for more soccer tennis and small-sided games and maybe some more strength training. "Sometimes we'd go out and watch the older guys play for a little bit if our training was after theirs," Trevor says. Then two more hours of training under the lights. "I would say that in the first six months I was there, I more than doubled the amount of soccer I played each day."

And that increase came against players far better than those he'd trained with in Orange County, including Carlos Salcedo, a future starter for the Mexican national team. "I played against Carlos in so many small-sided games outside of practice, and you could just never take the ball from this dude. He's easily the best player I've ever played against," Trevor says. "I think that was the biggest thing when I first got there, I got so much better, one, just from playing soccer more." Also, in Southern California he rarely faced players much older than him, whereas in Casa Grande he was regularly challenged by players two and three years his senior. "Having them smoke the shit out of you and embarrass you, those were little moments that I wouldn't have gotten."

It wasn't just that the players were more skilled or faster, it was also that they played differently. When he played in the Coast League in Orange County—"which is a little bit more of the wine-and-cheese crowd," Trevor says—he was playing with and against players who all trained the way he did and played the way he did. "I could go play in the Mexican leagues in Santa Ana and go against a different kind of player, but that's not going against them every single day," Trevor says. In Casa Grande, there was a Sergio Agüero type, the dynamo striker. There was a midfielder who reminded Trevor of Sergio Busquets—really shifty, not super pacey, but a player who would put in a crunching tackle. Then there was a guy so silky-smooth on the ball that Trevor thought of him as the team's Xavi.

In Casa Grande, there were film sessions, something that Trevor rarely experienced at his previous clubs, and he was asked to think about the game in a way he hadn't before. "I had my first real conversations about tactics and how teams defend and how to break down different teams, and just being a little bit more cerebral and deliberate. Before it was just like, 'Oh, yeah, some teams play with a 4-3-3. Some teams played 4-4-2,' and that's kind of it. Then I get to RSL and they are talking about the distance between players, and which shoulder you're standing off of at center mid, and how many times you're checking your shoulder. Those were the first times where anyone had ever pointed those things out to me."

The makeup of the players at RSL Academy was, by Trevor's estimate, about 30 percent white, 30 percent Latino, and 40 percent Black or Asian or another ethnicity. Many were scholarship kids, and others, like him, were paying to be there. "Freddy and the rest of the staff created a really good culture in the sense it really all came down to how good you are. If you're someone on scholarship, or if you were someone people knew was paying a lot of money to be there, if you were a baller, no one thought twice about that. It only mattered how good you were."

How much Trevor improved in his first year in the RSL Academy is best measured by what happened about ten months after he moved to Casa Grande: He committed to play at Stanford. He had been looking at mostly Ivy League schools and UC Irvine when he entered the academy, but after less than a year, his play elevated to the point that one of the nation's top programs wanted him. (Jordan Morris, a future MLS and USMNT player, was in his freshman class.)

"At RSL, you are just being tested in all these different ways hundreds of times a day. I knew guys who would wake up and they're like, 'My goal today is to touch the ball a thousand times before practice even starts,'" Trevor explains. "Compare that to my friends back home. They're in the suburbs, living in a nice area where there is all this stuff to do. Irvine is paradise. You can go to the beach with your friends, so much fun stuff to do. But that's a quagmire. Because in paradise you can't re-create the environment and the laser focus that everyone had at RSL."

Nothing has had a greater impact on the development pipeline, on the quality of male players the U.S. is producing, than MLS franchises investing in academies and prioritizing the cultivation of young talent. In October 2017, before the World Cup qualifier in Couva, only three of the players called into the U.S. camp came from a domestic pro team's academy. Four years later, there would be thirteen called into the U.S. camp (and three more who were developed in pro academies in Europe).

FC Dallas, the Philadelphia Union, Atlanta United, L.A. Galaxy, and Real Salt Lake have been among the most committed MLS clubs, and as their academies have borne fruit, other franchises have increased their investment. Some MLS teams are now so fully committed to developing their own prospects that they don't use all (or any) of their picks in the league's annual SuperDraft. The Union, for one, didn't draft a single college player in 2020 and 2021.

"And you now see academy jobs pop up all the time, positions like video analyst, performance analyst, nutritionist," says John Galas, who left RSL to coach with the Portland Timbers in 2013. "It has evolved really quickly."

The pro academy model has also, slowly, begun to crack the stranglehold that Pay-to-Play clubs have long had on youth soccer. MLS academies don't charge fees—the academy in Casa Grande initially did because it was a partner-ship between Grande Sports World and RSL—and that has erased some of the dividing line. MLS teams want the most talented kids and, although they might still scout too heavily in moneyed areas, skill is gradually becoming all that mat-ters. And the academy setup not only collects the best play-ers and places them with top coaches, it deepens the pool of players overall. The best youth clubs fill the spots vacated by kids who move on to MLS academies, creating more oppor-tunities down the line.

The RSL academy in Casa Grande was, by most mea-sures, a success, a groundbreaking proof of concept that a residency academy could work in the United States. But in 2015, the complex's owners and RSL leadership agreed to a mutual parting. The next year, RSL announced plans to con-struct a $50 million training complex in Herriman, Utah, a suburb of Salt Lake City. When that facility finally opened in 2017, the final price tag was $78 million. With 70,000 square feet of performance training and office space and 210,000 square feet of artificial playing surface, it was the largest such facility in MLS. The Zions Bank Real Academy, as it would be named, also featured the largest free-span structure—spanning 525 feet—in North America, covering an indoor field. It became the training hub for RSL's first team, the Utah Royals of the NWSL, and for the Utah Mon-archs of the United Soccer League Championship, which is RSL's reserve team.

Most crucially, RSL centered its youth academy at the complex, and that included housing for the young players and a charter school that owner Dell Loy Hansen, who'd made his fortune in real estate development, vowed would be the "Harvard of soccer." (Hansen's financial commitment to youth development had been unmatched in MLS, but his tenure as RSL's owner ended in disgrace. In 2020, he criticized his players for refusing to play after the police shooting of Jacob Blake in Wisconsin. *The Athletic* then published an article detailing racist remarks Hansen had allegedly made over several years. Not long after, the NWSL's Utah Royals were shuttered and Hansen put RSL up for sale, calling it "the best way forward" for the franchise.)

In 2017, when the academy in Herriman opened, David Horst, then thirty-three, was entering his ninth MLS season and had signed on for a second stint with RSL. He had played for the team from 2008 to 2010, so he was with the franchise just as the academy in Casa Grande got started, and then returned just as the Zions Bank Real Academy opened.

Toward the end of Horst's first stint, in 2010, RSL signed seventeen-year-old Luis Gil, a Californian coming off a strong U-17 World Cup. His signing was a big deal; Arsenal was rumored to be after him, and he was put straight into the first team, which at the time was unusual, given that Gil was a teenager. The year Gil was acquired, Horst remembers going to Casa Grande for preseason training. "It was in the middle of nowhere," he says. "They were still trying to build it up, get going, and there wasn't really any connection between the first team and the academy players down there."

Gil would go on to make 134 appearances over five years with RSL, but despite his early talent, he never became a star. In 2021, he played second-division soccer in the Czech Republic. "Gil is someone who might have been better off sitting in an academy for a few years," Horst says. "But that opportunity didn't really exist for him."

In 2017, when Horst returned to Salt Lake after stints with the Portland Timbers and Houston Dynamo, everything had changed. "When the academy moved to Herriman, you had those kids seeing us train every day, seeing professionals being professionals, and having a facility available to them 24/7," Horst says. "That year, you really saw the group of better players that you knew had a chance to be professionals increase. . . . In the mornings they would get to practice with us. So they're fourteen, fifteen, sixteen years old and getting to train with a professional team, and it was just an unbelievable situation for them."

Horst retired after the 2018 season but stayed on as an RSL academy coach. RSL mines Utah, California, Arizona, Nevada, New Mexico, and elsewhere for players. It also has a feeder program—RSL Arizona—based in Phoenix that is one of the biggest youth clubs in the United States; its recreational program alone is 3,000 kids.

In 2018, Horst was a technical director for the academy, focusing on kids under fifteen, and he and other coaches would monitor players all the way down to U-8. "Our job was to go out and scout all the youth players in Utah, find the players that we think had potential or an opportunity to maybe be a part of our academy," he says. They would bring in the top twenty kids, from U-10 up to U-13, and also track the next best forty kids in each of those age groups. "And then, when it came time for them to take that jump into the academy, then they went to the tryouts and we gave the Real academy staff our evaluations on the kids. The best RSL Arizona kids would come up to the tryouts as well. And it's a mixture of those two groups and whoever else they had scouted throughout the nation that would try and make the academy."

From 2017 to 2019, Horst would see the fruits of a commitment to youth development. Sebastian Soto, who played for the San Diego Surf, joined RSL's academy in 2016 when he was fifteen. Another talented fifteen-year-old, Taylor Booth, from Eden, Utah, joined the academy around the same time. Richy Ledezma was from Phoenix, and he moved to RSL's academy in 2016 at age fourteen. "It was exciting because you could see these were players that were not far away from being able to help the first team," Horst says.

Around the same time, in early 2016, Pulisic debuted for Borussia Dortmund as a seventeen-year-old and dazzled. Teams in Europe woke up to the fact that America had talent to be mined. Scouts from clubs in England, the Netherlands, Germany, and elsewhere began watching Development Academy games, eyeing the young players MLS teams were cultivating.

Many of those players were not contractually tied to a professional team, and the European teams pounced. Weston McKennie, who spent seven years in the FC Dallas academy (starting in 2009 when he was around eleven), rejected a Homegrown contract with Dallas and signed with Schalke 04 in Germany, which sent a shock wave through MLS front offices. Other talented young players followed McKennie's lead, rejecting the cut-rate Homegrown contracts for more lucrative deals in Europe. RSL lost Booth and Soto to teams in Germany (Bayern Munich and Hannover 96), and Ledezma to PSV Eindhoven in the Netherlands. Three players from Brian Kleiban's group left the Galaxy for European teams. "Everyone kind of woke up and said, 'Wait a minute, this is not good business,'" Horst says of MLS. "We're developing these kids and they are never playing for us, and we're not getting to sell them."

It took some time, but MLS owners began ponying up to keep young talent, "and so now we are seeing these players signing pro contracts and they are fourteen and fifteen and sixteen," Horst says.

In 2018, during his annual state-of-the-league address, MLS commissioner Don Garber pointed to the sale of elite young players Alphonso Davies (from Vancouver to Bayern Munich) and Tyler Adams (from the New York Red Bulls to RB Leipzig in Germany) as a model for other MLS clubs to follow. "We need to become more of a selling league," Garber said. "We've been buying for so long. But as we've gone through the analysis, it's hard to justify the investment we've made in players and the investment we've made in domestic development. We have to have something that turns the model around."

In the past few years, the model has flipped completely. FC Dallas embodies this the most, scouring for kids all over Texas and elsewhere, developing them, and then signing them to pro contracts. The team sold Reggie Cannon (to Boavista in Portugal), Bryan Reynolds (to Roma in Italy), Tanner Tessmann (to Venezia in Italy), Chris Richards (to Bayern Munich), and Ricardo Pepi (to FC Augsburg in Austria). And FC Dallas didn't empty its pipeline in the process. In 2021, the team still featured several Homegrown Players on its roster. The Philadelphia Union is another club active on the transfer market, moving three players to Europe (including USMNT regular Brenden Aaronson) for a return of around $12 million. The Union's total player payroll in 2021 was $10.5 million.

In the Project 2010 report that came out in 1998, a youth academy system tied to MLS teams was one of Carlos Queiroz's recommendations. It would have been nice if the leaders at U.S. Soccer had pushed for it back then, or after the Americans went winless at the 2006 World Cup. But capitalism eventually did the work for them.

In 2021, the RSL first team included three players—goalkeeper David Ochoa, center back Justen Glad, and right back Aaron Herrera—who came out of its academy. In January 2022, fourteen-year-old Axel Kei signed a two-year contract with RSL, becoming the youngest player to ever sign with an MLS team. Kei was born in Ivory Coast, raised in Brazil, and then moved to San Diego in 2017 when he was about ten. He played for an L.A. Galaxy affiliate in San Diego before moving to the RSL academy in Herriman. Kei is unlikely to help RSL win games anytime soon, but his signing highlights how RSL (and the other MLS clubs) now truly understand their place in the development pyramid. They find young talent. They cultivate it. They secure it with a pro contract. And when the time is right, they move it on for a profit, using some of the returns to find the next young star.

What became of Casa Grande, that impressive soccer complex in the desert that in 2015 saw its MLS partner exit?

After RSL left, a club you might have heard of—FC

Barcelona—approached the Casa Grande owners and proposed hosting a residency academy at the Arizona site. From afar, the endeavor looked like little more than a money-making opportunity for Grande Sports World, with some kids paying a reported $70,000 a year to attend the academy, and a marketing opportunity for Barcelona. But Barcelona sent two coaches to live in Arizona to augment the staff hired by Grande Sports World, and players follow the same curriculum as prospects at Barcelona's La Masia. The best players at the Arizona site also get to travel to Barcelona to be trained and evaluated by the staff in Spain.

In 2017, the year the Barça Residency Academy in Casa Grande opened, another Orange County kid was looking for a new club. Matthew Hoppe had made the Galaxy academy at thirteen but was cut after a year. He played two seasons for Strikers FC (Trevor Hyman's former club in Irvine, which had been renamed) but sought a more demanding environment and became one of the first kids to join the Barça Residency Academy. He initially didn't wow the coaches, but they moved him from the midfield to higher up the field, and he thrived as more of a pure goal scorer. He had twenty-nine goals for a U-17 team that reached the semifinals of the DA championship. That team also included Julián Araujo, from Lompoc, California, who chose the Barça Residency Academy over the lengthy commute required to train with the Galaxy academy. Those two players also got to share the field with the best young players at La Masia during a trip to Spain, a group that included Ansu Fati, who has since become one of the top young players in the world.

In June 2019, after two years at the Barça Residency

ademy, Hoppe signed with Schalke. A year later, he debuted for that German club and then in January 2021 scored
a hat trick, the first American to do so in the Bundesliga.
That summer, he started for the USMNT in a Gold Cup
quarterfinal, scoring in a 1–0 victory over Jamaica. In a
seven-year stretch, he had gone from being cut by the Galaxy
academy to starring on the national team, something he
could never have achieved had there not been a residency
academy option available to him. (Araujo, meanwhile, signed
a professional contract with the Galaxy in 2019 and two
years later was an MLS All-Star.)

"Are we getting the right players in these academies all
the time? Probably not," says Galas. "But there is at least a
real effort now. And just being a country that has an academy system and is working to get good players into a pro
environment? Well, that's a start."

THE BRIDGE

Embracing all the players the U.S. has to offer

It began in a warehouse under the Bay Bridge in San Francisco, which might bring to mind the tech startups of the 2010s: stylish spaces with glass walls and standing desks, a Ping-Pong table over to the side, locally sourced muffins and kombucha on tap in the communal kitchen, bright-eyed twentysomethings wearing designer sneakers, talking boldly about how they are reshaping the future while whispering about what they will do with their money when the IPO comes.

This startup, in 2002, was far from that.

First, the warehouse was so close to the Bay Bridge that the noise of speeding cars was unsettling. The space the founders rented was a windowless box of about 300 square feet, so, while they couldn't see the cars, they could hear them and even feel them, the constant rumbling of traffic.

Discussions were had about needing to move, but it became something they just decided to live with. Freeway noise? What freeway noise?

Then there was the smell.

The warehouse had once been a soy sauce factory. So everything—or at least many important things, like the floorboards—smelled of old soy sauce. It was particularly bad in the elevator, as if the car had been soaked in the stuff for decades. Day after day. Up and down. Soy sauce. Soy sauce. Soy sauce.

Third, there were the founders. They were not particularly young or wide-eyed. Brad Rothenberg was thirty-eight and Richard Copeland was forty-one. A year earlier, Rothenberg was earning a nice salary organizing corporate events for companies like Visa. Copeland was a lawyer who ended up not liking many of the people he encountered working in law. He then shifted to sports marketing, having a lot of success in the golf space. They were the kind of guys, with wives and kids already or soon to come, who would normally have been leaning more into their existing jobs, climbing the corporate ladder, starting to consider the state of their 401(k) plans and opening college funds. Perhaps it would have made sense to leave those jobs for a startup with a big pot of funding, but the venture capitalists fueling this enterprise were their wives. Deena Fisher, Rothenberg's wife, worked for Creative Artists Agency; Susan Copeland, for Google. They were the money, and it was far from infinite. In the early days, Rothenberg and Copeland went on a trip to Texas and splurged on a steak dinner. "You can't spend *that* much on one meal!" Fisher told them after taking a peek at the books.

"It is crazy to think now about the opportunity cost," says Copeland, who had two sons, ages two and four, when they started in 2002. "The choice to go out on our own was really a bad business decision."

There was also one important element missing from this startup: a concrete sense of what it would do. There was no product, not even a solid concept of one. They could agree that doing something in sports marketing made sense given their backgrounds and connections, but what? They didn't totally agree on what they were starting in that warehouse under the bridge. Still, they asked their wives to support them as they quit well-paying jobs, rent them space in a former soy sauce factory, then fund them as they set out to build a business that would do . . . something.

It made some sense that they would find their way into soccer—Rothenberg is a famous name in U.S. soccer circles. Brad's father, Alan, a lawyer, was president of the U.S. Soccer Federation from 1990 to 1998, and chairman of the 1994 men's World Cup and 1999 women's World Cup. He also played a huge role in the founding of Major League Soccer; from 1996 to 1999, the winner of the MLS Cup received the Alan I. Rothenberg Trophy. Alan was honored by FIFA with its Order of Merit in 2006, and elected to the U.S. Soccer Hall of Fame the following year.

In his previous job, Brad had leveraged his last name. It opened doors, helped him land clients. But with this new company, it was not Rothenberg who pushed for them to get into soccer. Copeland had been looking at the numbers from the 2000 census, "and I don't think anybody really took note of the Hispanic numbers." He did some research to see which sports marketing companies were targeting Latinos and found one small shop, but little else. "In the back of my mind, I was thinking this is a space that we could own," Copeland says.

"Richard kept insisting this was the direction we needed to go," Rothenberg says. "He won me over."

They caught a small break when MLS hired them to organize and stage 4v4 tournaments in MLS cities. Called Futbolito, it was the first Spanish-language program any league in the U.S. had ever done. "MLS owned it but we ran it, and it was this flag that we got to wave," Rothenberg says. They worked hard to line up sponsors, any sponsors, for those tournaments. Copeland was the cold-caller—they dubbed their little space "the boiler room"—and when they managed to squeeze a little money out of a company, they would line up across from each other in that small space, run toward one another, and belly bump, the 5-foot-11 Rothenberg slamming into the 6-foot-3 Copeland. (Maybe that part *was* a bit like the stereotypical tech startup.)

The sponsors for Futbolito and similar early initiatives were typically big names—Panasonic was one—but the amount they invested was usually small. For the first couple years, "we wrote far more checks than we cashed," Copeland says.

As a result, they traveled the country on the cheap— think Best Western, not Ritz-Carlton—and the two shared a room to cut down on costs. One night, Copeland forgot his contact lens case, so he stored the lenses in a glass of water on the bedside table. "I woke up in the middle of the night and drank them," Rothenberg says. "We had an event the next day and Richard couldn't see a thing."

It was like that for the first few years, the company not breaking even but the two of them becoming more and more familiar with the Latino soccer market. During this time, they connected with Bill Strube, who was attempting to help unaffiliated Latino clubs connect online so they could more easily create tournaments and work together in other ways. Strube's company was called Alianza de Futbol (Football Alliance), and Rothenberg and Copeland believed in its mission enough to buy a stake in it. But when that initiative fizzled, they refocused Alianza on staging adult tournaments, and eventually youth clinics and youth tournaments, for Latino players.

"It was years and years of building trust in those communities," Rothenberg says. "Here we were, two white guys, and they were suspicious of us, and they were right to be suspicious. But we kept coming back, year after year, hiring local staff, paying local referees, paying all our bills."

At these events, Rothenberg and Copeland talked to kids and parents and coaches and club directors. They learned how Latino clubs were often denied affiliation, and thus denied access to the best leagues. They learned about the Pay-to-Play model and how it created two worlds of soccer in the United States. And they also learned, event after event, how many good Latino players were operating outside the development pipeline.

"It is also important to remember the federation's thinking around this time," Rothenberg says. Only a few years earlier, the USMNT had made the quarterfinals of the 2002 World Cup, in no small part because of the efforts of young players Landon Donovan and DaMarcus Beasley, who were both only twenty years old. They had been products of U.S. Soccer's U-17 Residency Program, which started in 1999 and took the twenty best young players in the country (as identified by U.S. Soccer scouts) and housed them at the IMG Academy in Bradenton, Florida. There they got the kind of intensive day-to-day training that, to that point, only existed in pro academies beyond U.S. borders. After seeing Donovan and Beasley thrive at the World Cup, why would the federation believe it needed to broaden its search for top players? "Historically, the people inside the offices of U.S. Soccer have been very defensive," Rothenberg says. "I think there are some people there now who are able to acknowledge shortcomings, but going back to when we started, the people within U.S. Soccer believed they were identifying all the best players."

Rothenberg noted that, despite being shut out of the U.S. soccer system, "the Latino community was still respectful of the system, even as it marginalized them." He and Copeland came to believe that they didn't need to create something new for that community, a new pathway, but rather find a way to shortcut Latinos into the existing one. "We decided to try to build a bridge that connected Latino players to MLS teams, to Mexican teams, to the U.S. soccer academy system," Rothenberg says.

This wasn't a lightbulb moment for Rothenberg. He and his father talked often about how U.S. Soccer neglected minority communities, about Pay-to-Play. Like Matt Carver in Iowa and David Keyes in San Diego, once you see the problem up close, and realize how sweeping and damaging it is, you can't unsee it.

During this stretch, the company started by two sports

marketing guys still working in that soy sauce warehouse became something different. One might say they (or their wives, really) became impact investors. But impact investing comes with the belief or expectation that generating a positive impact (be it socially, environmentally, or some other way) will also generate *some* return on investment. Rothenberg and Copeland decided to try to fix a problem while also knowing that it wouldn't lead to a windfall.

They had motivation and they had spirit, but how were these two guys in San Francisco, operating on a shoestring budget, going to fix a problem that had limited men's soccer in the United States for decades?

Proviso West High School is less than twenty miles from the Chicago offices of the U.S. Soccer Federation. In 2008, when Rothenberg, Copeland, and the small Alianza group gathered there, this went unnoted. It would take on greater significance later, when what they started just a short distance from the offices of the sport's power brokers would come fully into view.

Proviso West High is in Hillside, a diverse suburb that in 2008 was about 23 percent Hispanic or Latino and 43 percent African American. (Nearby Forest Park, in contrast, was less than 7 percent Hispanic or Latino.) This was where Alianza held the first event of a scouting program it named Sueño Alianza (Dream Alliance). The grand plan was to hold open tryouts around the country for Latino players, and get pro scouts there to see them. Chicago was like the beta stage of the project.

They identified two hurdles right away. The first was that

they had to get pro scouts to attend. Two sports marketing guys, even one with the last name of Rothenberg, didn't have much sway with pro teams. It helped that they were connected with Eddie Salcedo and his brother, Jorge—a former professional player in MLS and in Mexico, and a former UCLA coach. They were well-respected figures in the Latino soccer community. But even their vouching for the program only went so far. They found that scouts from Mexican pro clubs were far more receptive than those from MLS teams, "but we still had to pay them to show up," Rothenberg says. "Sometimes it was paying for travel expenses or, later at an event in Texas, it was that expensive steak dinner that my wife got on us about. We were doing whatever we could to get them there."

The other significant hurdle: How do you get the right players to turn out? They put out an open invitation for players under twenty-one, broadcasting it to the Latino clubs in the area they had previously worked with. "But we had no idea what we'd get," Rothenberg says. "There was a chance we were just going to get a bunch of old guys who just ignored the under-21 part."

Instead, hundreds of young players showed up.

The scouts they had enticed to that high school field were not from teams in the top tier of Mexican professional soccer, Liga MX, which probably worked in their favor. Two players from that tryout ended up landing contracts with professional teams in the second and third divisions of Mexican soccer. If it had just been Liga MX clubs, they might have been shut out. At future events in Houston and Los Angeles, Mexican clubs plucked a few more players, either signing them or collecting information on the youngest players to keep tabs on them for later.

Scouts from MLS and the U.S. Soccer Federation were another matter. "Brad knew [MLS commissioner] Don Garber," Copeland says. "He knew Sunil Gulati. He knew everyone. And we would invite U.S. Soccer people and MLS coaches and scouts, and no one would come out. It was like, are you fucking kidding me, we are doing all the work, and they won't even come look?"

Alianza trudged on. Copeland and Rothenberg bought out Strube, so they owned the operation outright. They landed deals with Allstate and Verizon thanks to some boiler room brilliance. That enabled them to hire a few more people and move up a couple floors to a bigger space in the soy sauce factory. They expanded the Sueño program to ten cities, eventually bringing the age limit down to eighteen. They created the national Sueño, held in Los Angeles each year, where the best kids from the other tryouts come together to be scouted.

As the scouting program grew, some of Mexico's biggest clubs noticed. When Marco Garcés, now the sporting director at Pachuca and a legendary evaluator of talent, heard about it, he responded: "Tell me when and where I need to be." And they didn't have to bribe him to get there.

Not everyone within U.S. Soccer was blind to the program's potential. At a federation meeting in the early years of the program, Rothenberg cornered Bob Bradley, the USMNT coach at the time. He told Bradley what they were doing and how the best players from each regional tryout would come together for a national tryout. "So you are going to determine who the best twenty-two are, and I only need to send a scout to see them?" Bradley said, shocked at how easy they had made it for him.

But Bradley didn't control U.S. Soccer's scouting operation, and for the first several years the federation treated what Alianza was doing as irrelevant. At one point, officials there told Copeland and Rothenberg they weren't even interested in having the U.S. Soccer brand visible at the events. Rothenberg and Copeland were marketers; they looked at the surveys and other data and knew they were involved with a community of players and parents with little or no connection to MLS or the U.S. national teams. They preferred Liga MX and Mexico. Even if the federation honchos didn't think much of the talent on the field, why couldn't they see the value in getting the U.S. Soccer brand in front of a passionate soccer audience? "It made no sense," Rothenberg says.

Perhaps it was just laziness or force of habit. U.S. Soccer scouts were used to looking in certain places (like the wealthy suburbs) for talent, and at that point only a few MLS teams were really beginning to place an emphasis on developing young players. It was still a league focused on buying ready-made talent. But at least some of the motivation for ignoring what they were doing, Rothenberg and Copeland believe, was more wicked. "Is it racism? Maybe," Copeland says. "If your mandate is to grow the game and you are just choosing to ignore a huge part of the population playing and embracing the game, well, I just don't know how you make that choice."

Perhaps you make it because making a different choice would mean admitting you were wrong. Alianza was doing more than just putting a bunch of Latino players on the field to be judged. They were challenging the belief, entrenched after the 2002 World Cup run, that the best players were already being found. That there was a substantial pool of talented players slipping through the cracks simply was not something the U.S.-based scouting community, most of them white Americans or white men from European countries, were willing to concede.

What would it take for them to change their view?

Says Rothenberg, "We just needed that one player who would really open everyone's eyes."

Jonathan González grew up playing in a cow pasture in Santa Rosa, California, next to the Kendall-Jackson winery, where roosters routinely ran onto the field. It was a perfect encapsulation of the haves and have-nots within the U.S. soccer system. In 2013, he was fourteen years old, immensely talented, living in an area full of wealth, and his team of mostly Latino players couldn't find a real field to train on.

González's club, Atletico Santa Rosa, wasn't part of the Development Academy, and thus not a natural stop for U.S. Soccer's talent evaluators. But while hiding in plain sight, he was spotted by Hugo Pérez, a former USMNT midfielder. Pérez was working as a technical advisor for the federation and, in addition to alerting U.S. Soccer officials about González, he approached Rothenberg: "How can we help this kid reach his potential?" Rothenberg plugged González into the Alianza tryout program, and he dazzled.

The culmination was the 2013 Sueño Alianza in Los Angeles. After his performance there, González, a midfielder, got contract offers from thirteen Liga MX clubs. It was notable who *didn't* make an offer: the San Jose Earthquakes. At the time, MLS teams were prohibited from scouting outside their Homegrown territory, meaning the Earthquakes were the only franchise that could have acquired González. And though the Earthquakes had started their youth academy three years earlier, that team (and MLS in general) had yet to fully embrace signing and developing young talent. Thus, for a player like González, his only real opportunity for a professional contract was with a Liga MX side.

Even after he joined Monterrey in Mexico, González played for the U.S. youth national team at several age levels. That was, in part, because of Pérez, who acted as a conduit between the federation and his family. Pérez was coaching the U-14 and U-15 U.S. national teams, but in 2014 he was ousted from that position. The reason has never fully been explained by either side. There were vague comments about disagreements over coaching philosophy between Pérez and more senior U.S. Soccer coaches. There were rumblings that he favored smaller (i.e., Latino) players too much for the federation's liking; for one camp in 2013, twenty-one of the thirty players Pérez called in were Latino. Journalist Will Parchman watched Pérez take a U-15 boys' team to the 2013 Development Academy showcase and play against three U-16 teams. Many of Pérez's players were thirteen, two years younger than some of their opponents. And his players got beaten, were dominated in stretches, but, no matter the score, Pérez had the team trying to build out of the back, and he saw the three-game gauntlet as proof they could do it. Looking back on that group of players, Parchman concluded about

Pérez, "He was, by a significant margin, the best thing to ever happen to USSF's youth system. And he was thrown to the curb. Politics."

Adds Rothenberg, "What people at U.S. Soccer won't admit, and if they did it would be only in a whisper, is that instead of firing Hugo they should have kept him and then tried to hire another fifty coaches like him."

Over the next few years, González progressed at Monterrey, and by November 2017, when he was still just eighteen, he was a starting midfielder—a huge developmental success for the Liga MX team, considering he had been plucked out of an independent tryout in Los Angeles. His ascent to pro starter came right around the time of the disaster in Couva, a silver lining of sorts for those hoping for a brighter future for the USMNT.

One month after Couva, the U.S. senior national team scheduled a friendly against Portugal and took an experimental roster of mostly young players, including many of González's peers in the pipeline with whom he had played on U.S. youth teams. But interim head coach Dave Sarachan didn't select González. That slight opened a crack for the Mexican federation. Technical director Dennis te Kloese flew to the U.S. over Liga MX's Christmas break and had dinner with González and his family in Petaluma, California. Mexican national team coach Juan Carlos Osorio also called González, laying out a clear vision for how he thought González fit what the national team was doing.

The USSF was not blind to what was happening, but its response was limited. Rothenberg had grown close with González and his family, and he felt as if he was the only person trying to get González to stick with the U.S. "He was a kid who grew up wanting to represent the U.S., and it stayed that way right up until the moment he chose Mexico," Rothenberg says.

González may never be a player on the level of Weston McKinnie or Tyler Adams or other USMNT midfielders around his age, but he was talented enough that his decision to go with Mexico in January 2018 shook a lot of people. The blame fell mostly on Thomas Rongen, who was chief scout under Bruce Arena and had been tasked with trying to keep González in the red, white, and blue. Rongen didn't help his cause when he gave an interview in which he falsely claimed to have visited González's home three times to persuade him to stay, and then painted González's choice as a sort of inevitability. "His dad is so Mexican that he wanted him to represent Mexico, and I knew it was a losing battle, probably," Rongen commented to CBS.

But blaming Rongen is like focusing on lineup choices after the failure in Couva; it misses the forest for the trees. "I've known Thomas since my dad owned the Aztecs in the NASL," Rothenberg says. "He is a good person. It was the federation's decision to have a white Dutch American in his sixties try to develop a relationship with a Mexican American family in Santa Rosa."

The González saga brought more attention to the battle Rothenberg and Copeland were fighting. One year before González chose Mexico, Rothenberg says that Tony Lepore, the USSF's director of talent identification, notified Alianza that the federation would no longer scout Alianza events because they hadn't yet found any elite players at them. Then

González, who emerged from an Alianza event, chose Mexico over the U.S. in part because of that kind of apathy toward the Latino community.

It was October 2019, and the setting was once again the Sueño Alianza national event in Los Angeles. Among the fifty or so under-eighteen players there was David Zavala, a sixteen-year-old from Grand Rapids, Michigan. He played for a club outside the Development Academy, and before that moment had been completely unknown to the U.S. Soccer Federation. But while being coached by Hugo Pérez and watched by scouts from clubs in MLS, the United Soccer League (USL), and Liga MX, Zavala shined; he was clearly the top talent there, and pro teams began contacting him.

Klaas de Boer, a scout for the U.S. youth national team program, read about Zavala's star turn at the Alianza event in *Soccer America*. He then contacted a regional scouting director in the Midwest, urging him to help come up with a plan to get Zavala into the U.S. development pipeline. Ponder that for a moment: U.S. Soccer learned about a talented sixteen-year-old because a scout happened to be reading *Soccer America*.

In many ways, Rothenberg and Copeland have stopped caring about what the USSF does. The federation has, Rothenberg says, largely punted on the idea of playing a big role in the development of Latino players. Scouts from U.S. Soccer can now be found at Alianza events, but Rothenberg considers them largely irrelevant. At a recent Sueño in Philadelphia, a federation scout approached Rothenberg and asked, "Are any of these players national team–ready?" It got Rothen-

berg's blood boiling. "Was Landon Donovan national team—
ready the first time they scouted him?"

There *are* signs of progress. MLS teams, now free of
Homegrown boundaries, can sign any players they want,
and league scouts are now regulars at Alianza events. The
number of Latino players in MLS and USL academies has
risen considerably. And Liga MX teams are being even more
aggressive in recruiting young talent from the States. The
pro teams in North America now see a real benefit to scouting and developing Latino players. Rothenberg is enthused
by these developments but still laments how little the federation has done to bring about this change.

"It is an approach designed by neglect," he says.

The Alianza guys keep working to combat that neglect
and now have fifteen full-time employees dedicated to various programs. In 2016, they started a Sueño program for
girls, and they've expanded to helping Latino players get into
college with an initiative called Access U. "You know how
rich families pay for all those services to help kids write college essays and those sorts of things? That is what we are
now doing for kids," Rothenberg says. Recently, they started
Black Star Initiative, which aims to grow the game in Black
communities; Patrick Rose, the former Howard player and
MIT student, was one of their first hires.

The two guys who started in that soy sauce factory under
the Bay Bridge weren't ever going to fix a generational problem so fully ingrained in the system. But while helping the
Latino players that they could, they defined the scope of the
issue. No longer can anyone say all the talented players are
being found, that there are no elite Latino kids slipping

through the scouting net. In a way, they also defined the vast potential of men's soccer in the U.S., if it would embrace all the players between its shores.

That is something that, in Mexican soccer circles, is talked about often: What happens if the U.S. figures it out, fully utilizes *all* its talent? At a recent Sueño near San Jose, Marco Garcés from Pachuca addressed that topic with Joaquín Escoto, a vice president at Alianza.

"[In the U.S.] it is like they are trying to make Italian food but don't realize they have Mexican ingredients," Garcés said. "You need to look at what you have before you decide what to make."

IV

On a June day in 2015, nearly five years after Carver had founded the J-Hawk Soccer Club, he and his wife, Renee; daughter Jessi; and Edin Kazazic, a J-Hawk board member originally from Bosnia, arrived at the Des Moines Marriott for a grievance hearing in front of an arbitrator appointed by the USSF.

Carver had fundraised most of the $3,700 required to fight the Iowa Soccer Association's refusal to affiliate J-Hawk, and he paid the remainder himself. He had prepared so thoroughly for the hearing that, when he counted up the hours he had put into battling the ISA, he estimated that—if he had been hired to handle the case—he would have billed the client more than $10,000 in legal fees.

Entering the conference room, he was nervous. He had been a lawyer for fourteen years but rarely appeared before judges or took part in arbitration. "I'm more of a transactional attorney," he says.

The hearing took the better part of a day. ISA had hired an attorney and had what Carver estimated to be more than six hundred pages of exhibits. Both sides offered witnesses and the hearing was, at times, charged. ISA had a parent testify about the "chaos" created by J-Hawk's existence, the hard feelings between players and parents; one parent said there was so much drama created by the existence of the two clubs that his daughter considered switching schools. The dynamic was politely referred to as "tension" during the hearing, but everyone in the room knew it was more than that.

Cutting through the emotion, ISA's position rested on three pillars:

1. ISA has the right to impose subjective criteria for membership.
2. The Urbandale Soccer Club was already in the area, so J-Hawk was unneeded.
3. J-Hawk didn't offer anything unique that differentiated it from the existing club.

On Point 1, Carver knew he was going to lose. As long as the subjective criteria was "reasonable," ISA had the right to impose it. He also understood that if he could prove Point 3 was false, Point 2 would fall with it. The case would be decided on whether the arbitrator believed J-Hawk was different enough from USC.

Carver put forth evidence of J-Hawk's lower fees and its scholarship program that didn't require participants to provide financial information. His witnesses talked about how J-Hawk's coaches were all volunteer while some of USC's coaches were paid, and how J-Hawk's teams gave players the flexibility to play other sports. Carver shared a photo of his son Max's team and the number of first-generation Americans on it. "This is what we want to stop?" he asked loudly.

ISA's counter to those points was that it hadn't considered those issues when denying J-Hawk's application for membership.

One ISA witness testified that the presence of two clubs in Urbandale could create problems in the older age groups. If there were only, say, sixteen kids in a certain age bracket, and they were split evenly between J-Hawk and USC, neither club would have enough to field a team, thus denying all of the kids the chance to play. Sure, that is a concern, the arbitrator acknowledged, but it is only a concern if the clubs don't work together in those instances. And is that concern worth denying the now four hundred kids of J-Hawk an opportunity to compete in local leagues?

As for the "tension" the presence of two clubs in the community had created, the arbitrator asked whether that might have been exacerbated by ISA's rejection of J-Hawk's application. ISA had positioned itself as the protector of the status quo, and in doing so, it had branded J-Hawk as something foreign to be suspicious of.

At the end of the hearing, Carver was spent. Listening as officials from ISA, parents from USC, and others attacked his club, painting it as causing more harm than good, flattened him. He believed he was doing the right thing, but it still took a toll to hear so many people characterize him as the bad guy. That evening, back at home, he called J-Hawk board members and relayed how the hearing had gone, reliving the criticisms and allegations. Anger bubbled to the surface at times. Mostly, though, hearing people say out loud what he long knew they thought about him and his players just made him deeply, deeply sad.

A few weeks after the hearing, Carver was alone at Martin Field, in the 12-by-20-foot shed, about to get the mower out to cut the grass. He received an alert on his phone: An email had arrived from the U.S. Soccer Federation with the decision. "My heart started beating fast," he says.

He read the decision, and from the jump it was a clear repudiation of the Iowa Soccer Association's approach. One telling passage from the decision: "The existence of a second club in Urbandale did not, in fact, significantly weaken both clubs, or cause either of them to fail. To the contrary, both USC and J-Hawk have seen increases in the number of participants over the last several years."

Carver started pumping his fist, screaming. There he was, in that small shed, surrounded by corner flags and bags of beat-up balls, and five years of bottled emotion, of battling just so his kids could play in the same league as others, came pouring out. He shouted and jumped around and celebrated like he'd scored the winning goal in a World Cup final. Finally, someone had put down on paper what he knew to be true, what he'd been telling people for five damn years: J-Hawk's presence, its lower fees and unpaid coaches, its openness to all kids, was good for soccer. Good for Urbandale. Good for families.

He called his wife. He called a few parents from the club. He took a few moments for himself. Then he lugged the mower out of the shed and got back to work. That grass wasn't going to cut itself.

Not long after the USSF decision, ISA made J-Hawk an affiliate. No one there apologized for five years of obstruction that cost Carver thousands of dollars—money that could have been spent on scholarships or badly needed equipment—or for denying J-Hawk players a chance to compete on equal footing with other Iowa kids. Since the ruling, "Everyone at

ISA has been nothing but professional with us," Carver says. He even sent a letter to ISA's director thanking him for the organization's professionalism after the ruling.

But that professionalism, combined with the lack of repentance, also supports what Carver believed from the beginning: The obstruction was the point. ISA hoped to chill attempts to disrupt the Pay-to-Play model for as long as possible, to blunt a threat to "the establishment," as Matt's father had warned. No one at ISA ultimately saw what they did as harmful enough to repent. And, once forced to accept J-Hawk, they did so without (at least outwardly) holding a grudge.

Carver would later learn that before J-Hawk there had been other startup clubs—including one hoping to serve the area's Latino community—that had tried to break into the Des Moines soccer scene but, also denied affiliation by ISA, had quietly died. J-Hawk avoided the same fate only because Matt Carver happened to be an attorney, because he had the time and resources to fight, and because he was the son of Victoria and Mike, who taught him to use his privilege for good.

After the USSF ruled in J-Hawk's favor, club directors from other states reached out to Carver. Their clubs had also been denied affiliation, they told him. Across the country, established clubs and state associations were working to protect Pay-to-Play, even when it meant fewer kids had access to the sport. Carver helped those clubs that reached out to him, and anyone else who asked. He continued to operate J-Hawk and coach Rockne's team. (In March 2020, he took him to a tryout at RSL, where Rockne impressed but not enough to earn a spot in that MLS academy.)

In recent years, new youth clubs have started popping up in Des Moines. United Football Academy is a predominantly Latino club. Genesis Football Club's stated goal is to create "playing opportunities for immigrant and refugee youth"; many of its players are first-generation kids from Africa. Other clubs surfaced and began offering lower-cost elite programs.

When those new clubs applied for ISA affiliation, they were swiftly accepted. There was no attempt to protect the established clubs and Pay-to-Play. No ban. Because of Matt Carver, hundreds and hundreds more children are now playing soccer in Iowa.

EXPANDING THE PIPELINE
Turning America's vastness into an advantage

Liam O'Connell doesn't remember the player's name, but he remembers his talent.

The boy was around eleven or twelve when he came to the attention of O'Connell and others working for Sporting Kansas City (SKC). The drive, the technical ability, the requisite speed and agility, it was all there. The opinion of everyone from the MLS club who scouted the kid was: Get him on Sporting KC's U-13 academy team. Get him in the pipeline.

There was a problem, however. The boy lived in Omaha, Nebraska, 185 miles from where SKC's academy teams trained and played home games.

O'Connell joined SKC in 2012, when he was twenty-two years old, as the sporting club's network director. He had played soccer growing up in Hadley, Massachusetts, "middle of nowhere New England," as he put it, with forty-two kids in his high school graduating class.

His appeal to SKC was not his experience on the pitch or some deep knowledge of the tactical aspects of the game. O'Connell's strength was that he had an unwavering passion for the sport and a belief in its potential in America. He jumped eagerly into his work, which involved building up SKC's youth club affiliate program, connecting the pro club with youth clubs in the Midwest and South. At the time, there were no MLS teams in Minnesota or Nashville; there was no USL team in St. Louis. "We were on an island in the middle of the country," O'Connell says. "You had to drive at least eight hours in any direction before you got to another MLS city." The club's stated mission with its affiliate program was to connect with communities and help grow the game. So O'Connell did that. He met with club directors and coaches, brokering partnerships, finding ways the clubs could work together. But Peter Vermes, the sporting director and SKC coach, also posited this possibility to the SKC staff: "Could there be diamond-in-the-rough players in those communities?"

This Omaha kid was a potential diamond.

O'Connell and others from SKC connected with the boy's family and tried to craft a way for him to be part of the team's academy setup. "His family was really great. They wanted to do everything they could to support him," O'Connell says. "They tried doing the drive periodically, but his parents worked, and you are asking them to drive three hours each way multiple times a week." The boy thrived when he was with the other academy players and took to the coaching, but eventually his parents decided they couldn't make it work. "There was a point in time where the kid realized he wasn't going to be able to do this full-time, and it was heartbreaking," O'Connell says.

Over the next couple years, SKC's academy coaches would occasionally go to Omaha to host a camp or clinic. "And you bet that kid was first to register every time we were coming to town," O'Connell says. The player would also come to Kansas City for regional training programs, shorter training opportunities with SKC's top academy players. He was doing everything he could to get the best coaching possible. The only obstacle was geography.

When the boy was about fourteen, he made the trip to Kansas City for a training session. "He was now training with kids who had been in our training environment, been at this higher level with higher-level players, three to four times a week, for years," O'Connell says. "They just were learning at a faster rate and now you could really see it. They had passed him by."

The sheer size of the United States—both its general population (330 million) and the number of kids who play soccer (close to 4 million in 2020)—is often cited as a reason the country should be producing more elite players. But before (and even after) the formation of MLS academies, large parts of the U.S., including substantially sized cities, lacked a local training option—top coaching, elite teammates and opponents—that could push the most talented players to reach their potential.

Imagine if France largely ignored all the prospective players in Lyon. Or if England punted on prospects in Leeds. Or if Germany did the same with Dresden. Those cities are about the same size as Omaha, around 485,000 residents. For young players emerging from one of these forgotten U.S. areas, to get elite training meant moving with or away from your family, or strenuous commutes to practice multiple times a week. It also often required money, for gas, food, and other necessities. How, for example, would a single working parent manage the logistics and expense of driving a child three hours each way from Omaha to Kansas City several times a week?

Players in more developed soccer nations face these same hurdles; kids move from, say, Dresden to Dortmund or Munich in order to train with the best clubs in Germany. But there is an alternative. In most European cities of significant size, there are one (or more) local professional teams that also develop the area's best young players. In the U.S., there had been nothing for decades. Then there were fledgling MLS academies. Now there are growing MLS academies, but still far too few to cover the entire country.

It doesn't mean great players never emerge from these areas, including Omaha. In 2017, twelve-year-old Ozzie Cisneros from South Omaha, the youngest of five children whose parents immigrated from Mexico, began training in the SKC Academy. He commuted there with two other kids from the area. A year later, at thirteen, he moved to Kansas City, living with a host family. "I was afraid this was going to happen, even before it happened," his mother, Maria Guadalupe, told reporter Christopher Burbach of the *Omaha World-Herald*. "I had to overcome my fear of letting him go." At sixteen, he signed a professional contract with SKC.

In 2016, SKC scouted Gianluca Busio, who was playing for a club in Greensboro, North Carolina. He was fourteen, and his local club, the North Carolina Fusion, was one of the top clubs in the state. He was not exactly a hidden gem, but at the time there were not yet teams in Atlanta or Charlotte competing in MLS. O'Connell gave Busio and his mom a tour around SKC's stadium, selling them on the dream of playing there one day. Busio moved to Kansas City and a year later signed a professional contract with SKC. In 2021, at nineteen, Busio got a call-up for the Gold Cup with the USMNT and a short time later was sold by SKC to Venezia in Italy's Serie A, for a reported transfer fee that could rise to $11 million.

For the United States to maximize its population advantage, however, extraordinary steps—like those made by Cisneros and Busio (or the players who moved to Casa Grande)—cannot be the only way for top young players to get the training and environment they need. To deepen the pool of prospects, there has to be an alternative for those kids and families unable or unwilling to move or ship a child away or pay for costly commuting. That is what O'Connell concluded during the more than six years he worked for SKC, traveling the Midwest, connecting with coaches and families.

"Through that process," he says, "I realized, I'm recruiting twelve-year-olds from four to five, six hours away. And, at the time, the honest answer was that was their best shot at making it. But that shouldn't be the only answer."

It's a warm Thursday afternoon as Nick Evans walks from Toyota Field and a first-team practice, across a parking lot, and into the San Antonio FC coaches' offices. The conference room overlooks the team's training grounds and the pristine grass fields. It is February, but February in San Antonio can bring perfect training weather, and this is one of those days. "We can pretty much train year-round here," Evans says.

Evans is from Wales but has lived in San Antonio since 2006, when he moved there to play for the University of the Incarnate Word. He then coached at a local club before being tasked, in 2016, with helping coach the first team and growing San Antonio FC's academy.

San Antonio FC plays in the United Soccer League Championship, the second division of professional soccer in America. The USL also operates USL League One (third division) and USL League Two (fourth division). The simplest way of looking at the professional pyramid in the U.S. is that MLS controls the top league in America, but USL operates almost everything below that, a total of 127 teams as of 2021. (In 2022, MLS launched MLS Next Pro, a third-division league for mostly younger prospects.)

Among the thirty-one franchises in the championship are teams in cities that likely could (and someday might) support an MLS team, such as San Antonio, Las Vegas, and San Diego. The twelve teams in League One and eighty-four in League Two are from smaller locales: places like Madison, Wisconsin, and Tucson, Arizona, in League One; and Wichita, Kansas, and Little Rock, Arkansas, in League Two.

San Antonio's population (1.4 million in 2020) is twice that of Omaha, and a majority (around 64 percent) identify as Hispanic or Latino. It is nearly a three-hour drive from

San Antonio to Houston and more than four hours to Dallas. Austin is closer to an hour, but that city only began MLS play in 2021—and that would still be a hellacious daily commute for soccer practice. San Antonio's ample talent pool has been mostly tended to by local Pay-to-Play clubs or Mexican professional teams, which pluck players out of Texas and take them south of the border to develop.

For America's development system to not reach Omaha is tragic; for it to neglect San Antonio is tragic *and* stupid. The city should have long been a soccer hotbed, pumping out professional players yearly.

"San Antonio has not had a strong, deep soccer history," Evans says. "It's had some very good players down the years, had some really positive coaches. But it's not been enough. I think it's based on the fact that for the most part, the level of accessibility for everyone wasn't great, because we were in a Pay-to-Play model for so long."

In 2020, when I sat down with Evans, San Antonio FC was entering its fifth year operating a youth academy and had totally flipped the script. The club had 103 full-time players on teams in U-12 through U-17. There were eighty more in their pre-U-12 track program, promising players who trained with the academy coaches on Monday nights and were being scouted as potential entries into the academy. And Evans and others from the club tracked an additional sixty or so part-time training players in various age groups.

The full-time players are fully funded: uniforms, travel, everything. "Because historically in this city, it's been very, very difficult for an academy program like this to survive and thrive," Evans says. "To start with, there are people with

low socioeconomic means, and we are also a geographic region with a degree of difficulty of traveling to certain loca-
tions. And then the commitment, and the consistency of the
quality of training, and all the other layers that come with
being a kid and stuff—it has been a challenge."

About 85 percent of the 103 full-time players are Latino,
many of them first-generation Americans. Given the cost for
San Antonio FC (SAFC) teams to compete in the Development Academy before it was disbanded in 2020 (and replaced
by a new youth super league, MLS Next) and then in the USL
Academy League—which involved trips to places such as California, Florida, Colorado, and elsewhere each year—Evans
estimates that fewer than 20 of the 103 kids could afford to
play if the team didn't cover expenses.

"We knew we had to create a program that had no barriers. We wanted it to be for everybody who was good enough
to be a part of this," Evans says. "We talk about firsts a lot
with our players. First time to travel, first time to get on a
plane, first time to go to Europe, first time to go to Mexico,
first type of food they eat, first hotel they've spent a night in.
A lot of our kids, they don't get to do some of this stuff if
they're not with us."

San Antonio FC's academy has completely transformed
the city's development structure. The connections that Evans
and others have built in the local soccer community have
helped defuse potential conflicts, so there are rarely disputes
over players. And what SAFC offers is simply so superior
that any local coach telling a player he shouldn't join the
academy or go to one of SAFC's identification events would

get laughed out of the room. The best kids in San Antonio now get the best coaching almost across the board.

Kids like Leo Torres. In 2016, at age twelve, he attended an SAFC identification event, one player in a sea of about a hundred. He was previously with a club called Lonestar SC, a good club, Evans says, "and he was doing really well at that club." But then SAFC brought him onto its U-13 team. "Each year he just got better and better," Evans says. In February 2019, Torres became the youngest player—and the first from SAFC's academy—to sign a professional contract with the franchise. He had turned fifteen less than a month before. By that point Torres had already caught the attention of national team scouts, and the midfielder had been called up to train with the U-15 U.S. national team.

SAFC didn't identify midfielder Jose Gallegos as early, but they were aware of him, scouting him continuously, and he eventually joined the team's academy as a high schooler. He turned down a scholarship to North Carolina State in order to sign a professional contract with SAFC in 2019. In 2021, after his first professional season with SAFC, as European clubs began to scout him, he went on trial with Bayern Munich and Barcelona, and was eventually sold to a Danish club.

Prior to the creation of SAFC's academy, Torres and Gallegos "maybe get spotted and go play in Mexico, maybe they go to college," Evans says. "If this doesn't exist, it's very difficult for them to reach their potential." One day in 2020 when we spoke, two other academy products had just begun training with the professionals inside Toyota Field. In U.S.

soccer circles, it is understood that SAFC's academy is better run and more productive than many MLS academies.

"There are some [professional] clubs in the U.S. who want to invest more money in certain parts of their program and in their club, but maybe not as much in the youth," Evans says. "But we have a responsibility to the youth, because ultimately, we can't just have players being developed better on the West Coast or on the East Coast, and in the Northeast, but not in the Southwest or in the Mid-Central. The more we can do as a country, developing young players properly, the more players we can get."

Evans then (perhaps unintentionally) channels ESPN's Taylor Twellman for a moment, echoing his famous rant about America's development system.

"It needs to be done at the city level, the club level, then it goes up to the league level, with the leagues getting better, and that helps everyone. And then it moves up to the national team level, and it improves there. But it starts with each [professional] team focusing and putting in the resources at the youth level. If we're not doing that, then really, what are we doing?"

In 2018, Liam O'Connell left Sporting KC. He wasn't unhappy—he liked his job, liked the people he worked with—but the belief that there must be another answer for how to develop American players had been gnawing at him for a few years.

O'Connell had talked to USL officials from time to time about the development landscape. Eventually, USL leadership recognized that it had a role to play that could help its pro teams *and* boost the country's ability to identify and develop top talent. O'Connell was hired as USL's senior director of youth development, and he led a charge to help USL teams build an academy to create professional pathways in places where they didn't exist before.

SAFC's Academy is the crown jewel of the USL developmental system, but there are other clubs finding success. Sacramento Republic FC helped develop local prospects Travian Sousa, Roberto Haṭegan, and Quincy Butler before those players joined professional teams in Germany. At the time they left, Sacramento Republic didn't have a pathway for those players to play with the first team. The youth team and pro team weren't connected. Now they are, and Sacramento Republic features several teenagers signed to professional deals, including the talented fifteen-year-old Rafael Jauregui.

The USL has standards for its clubs and how they structure their academies, but the franchises have some autonomy. They can seek out partnerships and take the approach that best fits their community. O'Connell isn't going to tell Nick Evans and the other SAFC coaches how to do outreach in San Antonio's Latino community. He is available if advice or support is needed, but there isn't a one-size-fits-all approach.

In 2019, Orange County SC (OCSC) in Southern California (a USL Championship team) entered into a partnership with Scottish power Glasgow Rangers. Among the initiatives, Rangers coaches assist in crafting and implementing training sessions for Orange County kids, allowing some OCSC players to train in Scotland. It is a partnership that, for Rangers, may be mostly about branding in the U.S. market, but it still creates an opportunity for Orange County coaches and players to get training they otherwise wouldn't receive. Goalkeeper Aaron Cervantes, who signed with OCSC as a fifteen-year-old in 2018, eventually broke into the club's senior team and was on the U.S. squad at the 2019 U-17 World Cup. After the partnership with Rangers was formed, Cervantes went to Glasgow for a trial, and impressed. In October 2020, he was sold to Rangers in a deal that reportedly could net OCSC high six figures, money that conceivably will be put into developing the next Cervantes.

"Rangers recognizes there is a pathway to bring American talent to Europe, and the USL and a club like OCSC found a way to make it mutually beneficial, for it to be a fan and player development opportunity," O'Connell says. "The thing behind the scenes that is the biggest development is the technical benefits. The new opportunities for player and coach development are significant."

In spring 2021, play started in the USL Academy League, an initiative O'Connell spearheaded to help further professionalize youth development in the older age groups. The plan is for each of the teams in the USL Championship, League One, and League Two to effectively create a reserve team of younger players. There is a limit on the number of U-18 and U-19 players a team can have, and a minimum for players U-17 or younger. The setup essentially forces USL teams to create a reserve youth team just below its senior team; and because the Academy League's calendar aligns with the USL Championship and USL League One seasons (spanning March to November), the youth players will have more opportunities to train and play with and against professionals. The impact could be significant: In March 2021, in the first season of the USL Academy League, eight players from the SAFC Academy League team played in a friendly against FC Dallas. A few months later, ten SAFC Academy League players took the field versus Club Querétaro of Liga MX.

The USL Academy League will have a significant impact in League Two, which historically fills its team with current college players. More and more, League Two sides are playing local teenagers, and having a development team will only increase that. Those teenagers are then scouted by League One and Championship sides and brought in by teams a tier or two higher, and some of those young players are then choosing to skip college to sign professional contracts. Some USL clubs that were rivals are now banding together, forming development plans for the kids in their area. O'Connell brokered one such arrangement with League Two side AC Connecticut and Championship team Hartford Athletic. Another formed between the Tampa Rowdies of the top division and Tampa Bay United a tier below, with those clubs now linking up to find the best pathway for individual players in both clubs.

It is unlikely that in the coming years individual USL Academy teams will match MLS academy teams in terms of volume of truly elite young players, but that is not the goal. The goal is to fill in the gaps, to develop players outside of MLS areas that aren't being given an opportunity now. Says

O'Connell, "USL may have a greater impact on the trajectory of youth development in this country because of our scale. I truly believe this is the model that will solve American soccer."

Within the three levels of the USL, a somewhat consistent shuffle happens: teams coming and going, new teams founded, others folding. In 2020, when Major League Soccer announced plans to create a reserve league, a few USL Championship teams ceased operations, presumably to resurface in that league. That same year, COVID-related costs led to the demise of USL Championship franchises in Reno and St. Louis. Meanwhile, new teams popped up, and the expansion fees continued to rise, indicating that despite the shuffle, USL remains in ascent.

Among the teams that made their debuts in the USL in 2020 was one dear to O'Connell's heart: Union Omaha.

In 2019, Gary Green, owner of the Omaha Storm Chasers (a Triple-A baseball franchise he bought from Warren Buffett), led a group that brought a USL franchise to Omaha. Jay Mims, the coach at the University of Nebraska Omaha who also previously worked for Real Salt Lake, was hired to coach the team.

Before Union Omaha debuted in League One in 2020, Mims began reaching out to the youth clubs in Omaha and emailed the parents of the thirty to forty kids in the regional pool. He broadcast that the inaugural USL Academy Cup was coming up in San Antonio in a few weeks, and he wanted to know if any kids would be interested in going. The USL Academy Cup was, unfortunately, the same weekend as the Nebraska State Cup, a big deal for players. Mims wanted to know whether, if a player was selected for Union Omaha's USL Academy Cup team, they would be willing to skip State Cup to make the trip to San Antonio.

Every parent responded that their son would be willing to miss State Cup, because they recognized the golden opportunity Mims was offering their children.

Mims held a training camp, evaluating the fifteen- and sixteen-year-old kids, and selected sixteen to go to San Antonio. It was in many ways a perfect cross-section of all the talent Omaha had to offer—Mims purposely chose kids from different clubs and high schools. And Union Omaha's ownership group paid for everything. Before there was a Union Omaha senior team, there was an academy team, with the hope that this would be the beginning, that Union Omaha would eventually feature a fully funded USL Academy League team.

USL officials interviewed coaches and players from several teams for a video documenting the inaugural USL Academy Cup, and there is one moment from that video that O'Connell has watched too many times to count. It inevitably leads him to think back to that kid in Omaha from years earlier who slipped through the cracks, the one who had all the talent but lost his chance due to geographic hurdles.

In the video, one of the Union Omaha players, Yoskar Galván-Mercado, who has tousled brown hair and a bulbous nose and could easily pass for thirteen, explains how cool it was to be in San Antonio for the tournament—"I never thought I'd get out of Nebraska," he says—and then remarks that he hopes being there gets him and his teammates more exposure, so maybe a better college will recruit them. The videographer then asks, "And maybe go pro?" Says O'Connell, "And then there is like a glint in his eye, and he smiles and you can see it, like he realizes right at that moment that it could happen; that could be his dream."

CONCLUSION

On March 30, 2022, the final day of qualifying for the 2022 World Cup, Liam O'Connell's mind was in two places.

He was at his home in Tampa, with the television on, getting ready to watch the USMNT play in San José, Costa Rica. But by 5:00 A.M. the next day he had to be at the nearby Hillsborough County Tournament SportsPlex preparing for the USL Academy Cup, the biggest event of the year for USL youth teams. As he watched the U.S. finish out qualifying, he also tended to last-minute details for the days of games between players in the U-13, U-15, and U-19 divisions. "Here I am trying to deal with this huge logistical challenge," he says, "and I'm also nervous watching the national team because, after what happened in 2017, you just never know."

Similar to Couva nearly four and a half years earlier, qualification seemed a foregone conclusion. The U.S. was in second place and did not even need to win (only to lose by a smaller margin than 6–0) to get one of the three automatic qualifying spots. But the U.S. was without several key players due to injuries. The ghosts of Couva were still swirling as the team took the field.

But the game passed with minimal drama.

The U.S. struggled against a physical opponent on the road, and there was plenty to pick apart if one wanted, but the result, a 2–0 loss, was an emotional walk in the park compared to Couva. "In the second half, when it was clear Costa Rica had kind of given up hope, that's when I felt like it was okay to relax," O'Connell says.

One might have expected USMNT star Christian Pulisic to be overjoyed. After the disaster in 2017, Pulisic had crouched down and cried into his jersey, a lasting image of the lowest moment in U.S. soccer history. But rather than excitement or satisfaction or even relief, in a postgame interview Pulisic expressed annoyance. He didn't try to hide how perturbed he was that the U.S. hadn't qualified with a win. The interviewer attempted to get him to reflect, to loosen up, but he wasn't going for it. He was polite, but he was clearly pissed off.

Studio analysts Clint Dempsey and Oguchialu Onyewu (both former USMNT players) expressed the same sentiment. They weren't going as far as shouting "What are we doing!" à la ESPN's Taylor Twellman in 2017, but they also weren't settling for the redemption narrative.

"I loved how mad Pulisic was because he knows, and we all know, that the U.S. should not be backing into a World Cup with a loss," O'Connell says. "And it shouldn't be enough to just qualify. Yes, because of 2017 we might feel that way right now, but the U.S. should never be going into the last day of qualifying not having already qualified. And Dempsey and [Oguchialu] were saying the same thing. As a country, we have too much talent and too much potential for that."

The next morning, O'Connell would see that talent and potential on the field. The level of play of USL Academy teams has risen each year, with more clubs creating academies and the existing clubs improving at identifying and developing talent.

The surest sign that is true? The dozens of pro scouts from European clubs who attended the event. The second tier of professional soccer in America is now seen as so bountiful that clubs in Europe are tracking youth players from there with regularity.

"In the next five to ten years, the U.S. will become one of the top global producers of talent," O'Connell predicts. "It is going to be Brazil, France, and USA who are the leading producers of players who play in the top leagues in the world. Move ahead ten years and we are going to have ten Pulisic-level players in the Champions League."

Two players who appeared in the USL Academy Cup made their pro debuts with USL teams the week after the tournament. And remember the kid from Omaha, the one in the video who suddenly realized he might have a pro pathway? In the summer of 2021, Yoskar Galván-Mercado became Union Omaha's first homegrown signing. He once dreamed of going to a better college. Now he's a professional player. (And USL will cover his college tuition in a partnership with Bellevue University.) Nary a month passes without news of a young American signing with a domestic or European-based professional team. The week before the Costa Rica match, sixteen-year-old Adrian Gill from Colorado signed with Barcelona. Another sixteen-year-old, goalkeeper Diego Kochen, was already at La Masia. Both players have appeared for U.S. youth national teams.

"I loved that when Adrian Gill signed with Barcelona he said one of his goals was to start at the 2026 World Cup," O'Connell says. "It may not be him, but there are going to be many players that people haven't heard that much about who are going to emerge over the next few years."

There are still many flaws in the system.

One director from a French professional team disclosed to O'Connell after watching the U-13 players that they were better than the boys in France in that same age group. "But he said that was not true at the U-19 group," O'Connell says. That could be read two ways. The first: The younger generation of players are just better. The second: The U.S. is doing something wrong developing players as they move up the ladder. "Both may be true," O'Connell says.

Latinos also remain underrepresented on the national team.

While the USMNT is the most diverse it has ever been, with far more Black players featuring under coach Gregg Berhalter (though most of them were developed in Europe), only two or three Latino players were predicted to make the World Cup roster.

"The pool of players has become more diverse overall. It is not just rich white kids anymore, which is progress," says David Keyes, a decade after he first started studying immigrants and soccer. "But the wave of Latino players is probably a cycle away. I track the youth national teams, and what you see at the younger levels are rosters that have many more Latino players." To that point: Latino players made up nearly a third of the players called into a U.S. U-20 national team camp a few weeks after the Costa Rica game.

As I watched the U.S. men secure qualification in San José, it occurred to me that the USMNT had reached what could be considered the second phase in its ascent to becoming a true soccer power. Couva was the last gasp of the old system, the realization that to continue to identify and develop players the old way wasn't working. Now the new way is beginning to pump out more and better players. But the pipeline is still not operating at maximum efficiency.

The U.S. still isn't identifying all the talent between its shores; coaching remains inconsistent, particularly the farther you get from MLS and USL academies; too many people still act out of self-interest rather than do what is best for young players. But the fact that this pool of players is so much deeper and more talented than any before it shows how quickly the U.S. can rise.

As for Qatar, it is wise to remember the warning Carlos Queiroz gave in Project 2010: Don't overreact to one set of results, one tournament. If the U.S. went to Qatar and lost three group games, how should that be interpreted? Similarly, if the young American team won its group, if it advanced in the knockout stages, what would that mean in the bigger picture?

The U.S. team picked to go to Qatar is one of the youngest, if not the youngest, in the tournament; the average age of its core players is under twenty-five. Those two factors— youth and a lack of elite players beyond a handful of starters— leave the USMNT more susceptible to the whims of the game. An injury to a key starter could derail the U.S. this time around.

But in the future, if the progress happening in player development continues, the U.S. will likely have another such star ready to come off the bench. What might be seen as a setback now will be merely an opportunity for an equally gifted player.

"There is this momentum now," O'Connell says, "this collective energy that didn't exist before, where everyone is working and there is this embrace of this culture of development. It is not that we are meeting expectations. We are already starting to exceed them."

ACKNOWLEDGMENTS

This book doesn't happen without the support of my wife, Sharon, who has held my hand through three such projects. She has her own ambitions, her own work, and yet she always carves out time to help me find my way. As my daughter, Jessica, always says: "Mom is the *best* listener."

I benefited from the vision of two editors: Brendan Vaughan, who supported this book at its inception, and Emily Hartley, who did the hard work of making it better. Andrew Blauner, my agent, has been at my side for more than a decade and has never failed me. Claire Noland gave me notes that made every chapter better.

This book was largely reported during the pandemic, which meant that many people I spoke with, including Richard Copeland, Brad Rothenberg, Kab Hakim, Todd Beane, Patrick Rose, and others, had to provide me with more time than might have typically been required to properly flesh out their stories. I am grateful for their openness and patience. Spending time in Houston with Tom Byer and the academy staff of the Dynamo was inspiring, as was getting to witness what Nick Evans and San Antonio FC are building. In many ways, my vision for the book turned after talking to Liam O'Connell, as it clarified how quickly the development structure in the U.S. was shifting. Few people are doing more to change it than Liam.

Finding David Keyes's paper on boys' soccer in San Diego was a journalistic golazo, and David spent countless hours walking me through his research and talking to me about the history of youth soccer in America. I was beyond fortunate to have access to someone with his depth of knowledge and intelligence and passion for the game.

There are several people who may have appeared only briefly in these pages but who offered hours of insight that informed every chapter. John and Dave Galas, I can't wait to get back to Eugene and continue our conversations. I emerge wiser after each visit. David Horst now lives and coaches near where I live in Oregon, and I see him positively impacting a generation of kids weekly. Brian Kleiban and his brother, Gary, are somehow both insiders and outsiders within the U.S. system, and that made them fascinating subjects. They were initially reluctant to contribute to this book, but I am glad they chose to trust me.

There are many others with whom I spoke for this project—Steve Cherundolo, Nelson Larson, and Todd Kupka among them—whom I didn't end up writing about but who informed this project immensely. Thank you for your time and wisdom.

It was several years ago when I first learned what Matt Carver was doing in Iowa and what he was having to endure. That sparked the idea to report and write something larger about the U.S. men's soccer system. Matt would be the first person to tell you he is not perfect, but his wholehearted desire to make soccer accessible to young players no matter their race or gender or background or zip code inspired me.

Just before I started this project, I began coaching in and then later became president of the Ashland Soccer Club. I've coached two teams, a girls' team (the Dynamite) and then a boys' team (the Renegades). Coaching those teams and running the club has become an obsession. I am not obsessed with winning, however. What consumes me is trying to find ways that I can make soccer more accessible to the children in my community and how I can take what I learned working on this book and, somehow, give the ASC kids a perfect experience.

On the second point, I will fail. That I know.

But I hope that Jessica, Justin, Natalie, Audrey, Connor, and all the kids I have and will coach will be able to look back on their time playing for me and, at the least, say that no one tried harder than Coach George to help them find their place in the game.